365 DAYS OF AIR FRYER

Written by: Jamie Stewart

Copyright © 2016

All Rights Reserved

All rights reserved. No part of this book may be reproduced or transmitted in any form or by any means, electronic or mechanical, including photocopying, recording or by any information storage and retrieval system, without written permission from the publisher, except for the inclusion of brief quotations in a review.

Warning-Disclaimer

The purpose of this book is to educate and entertain. The author or publisher does not guarantee that anyone following the techniques, suggestions, tips, ideas, or strategies will become successful. The author and publisher shall have neither liability or responsibility to anyone with respect to any loss or damage caused, or alleged to be caused, directly or indirectly by the information contained in this book.

****

Download a FREE PDF file with photos of all the recipes.

Link located at the end of the book.

*****

Table Of Contents

Introduction

Have you ever wondered how to make "unhealthy" fried food in an easy and healthy way? Is that possible to enjoy the healthier version of your favorite foods such as French fries, burgers, cakes, or snacks? Many people struggle with changing their eating habits. There are so many diets, so many recipes, kitchen appliances, and so on. You're probably feeling overwhelmed by all those information, advice, and suggestions.

If you are trying to introduce healthy food options and lose weight, the situation is even more confusing. Here's the good news – you don't have to stick to any diet! Yes, you don't have to. Furthermore, your favorite foods are back on the menu! Just choose the right cookware and right cooking technique. That's it!

Hot air frying is the answer. An air fryer is simple but intelligent kitchen machine that use rapid air technology to cook food with less oil. As a matter of fact, this new cooking technique utilizes super-heated air to cook food in a specially engineered chamber. You will be pleasantly suppressed what air fryer can do for you!

Hot Air Frying:

A Surprising Way to Cook Your Food

Whether you are yet to buy an air fryer or you already own one, it is good to know its basic function and features. First and foremost, reading manufacturer's instructions for operation and cleaning is a must. Here are some of the most important air fryer features.

When your food is in the cooking chamber, superheated air is circulated around it to cook everything evenly. Thanks to its innovative features, you will be able to cook foods fast, easy, and more conveniently.

Then, air fryer has an automatic temperature control so you can be assured that your food will be perfectly cooked. Your air fryer makes great meals without a fuss.

Digital screen allows you to set your cooking preferences and enjoy the advantages of hands-free cooking. This is one of the best features of an intelligent kitchen machine.

Hot air frying machine does more than just fry. You can bake a wide variety of cookies, roast meat and vegetables, make the best puddings, etc. You can also add a grilling element for extra flavor and crispiness. Air fryer works more like a convection oven than a fryer. There are great air fryer accessories on the market like air fryer baskets, grill pans, baking pans, double layer rack with skewers.

We can use silicone, metal, or glass in most models. Nevertheless, always read machine's instructions before using any bakeware in your air fryer.

By all means, you will be able to get that deep-fried taste with only 1 tablespoon of oil. Therewithal, many argue that air-fried food tastes better. Air fryer allows you to make better food choices and you can have nutritious and great-tasting meals without the hassle.

An air fryer offers inspiration for many people to cook healthy and well-balanced meals every day. Hot air frying requires very little fat so that your meals retain most of their valuable nutrients.

Air is the New Oil

Many studies have now demonstrated that frying with oil can be harmful. Many common oils such as sunflower oil, soybean oil, corn oil, canola oil and a few others, contain huge amounts of Omega-6 polyunsaturated fatty acids, which are very harmful in large amounts. Then, those oils are loaded with trans fats that can be highly toxic. They increase our chance of developing various diseases, like diabetes, heart disease, cancer, obesity, and so on. Many studies linked increased Omega-6 intake to various diseases and degenerative changes.

If we use some traditional cooking methods such as deep-frying, we get food that is unhealthy and too fatty. On the other hand, baking is a healthier choice, but it is not suitable for many recipes. We want juicy and more flavorful food, right? Long story short, if you want to lower the risk of multiple diseases and eat better, then you should consider an oil-free cooking method.

Most of us are aware of the fact that we need tasty food that is prepared in a healthy and easy way. Making the switch to oil-free cooking is easy with air fryer. As we said before, air fryer uses super-heated air to cook food. And you can have fried fish fillets or fried breaded veggies right away!

When it comes to healthy eating, an air fryer is a great choice for you and your family. Why use an air fryer? There are lots of reasons to love the hot air frying:

Air is the new oil – you will use less oil. Most of recipes in this book call for 1 to 2 teaspoons of vegetable oil; the hot air circulates all around your food and you get surprisingly delicious food with all the natural juices.

Fans of fried food won't be disappointed – you will cook healthy meals while, at the same time, "fried" taste and texture is achieved. This means, we cut calories and bring more flavor to our food. Win-win!

Air-fried food is new fast food – actual cooking time is shortened because of the high temperature in the cooking chamber that is circulated all the time. Therefore, it's easy to speed up the cooking time. Cooking times will vary depending on factors like a type of your machine, a kind of food, the size of food and its thickness, etc. To avoid mistakes, test your food for doneness before removing it from the air fryer. Moreover, you can also cook two different meals but make sure to use the divider.

Safcty – air fryers are safe to use. You should only use your standard kitchen gloves to avoid injuries and burns. To avoid any troubles, consult your manual from time to time. Protecting our planet starts with you – air fryers are also environment-friendly.

The secret to getting more leisure time – the benefits of hands-free cooking are obvious as well. Just set your machine by choosing the right buttons and leave your air fryer alone. Therefore, you don't have to worry about stirring or burning, and checking the contents.

Recipes That Make Everything Better

Everyone who is lucky enough to own an air fryer and has an experience with this revolutionary cooking technique will enjoy this recipe collection. In this cookbook, you will have an amazing opportunity to explore the surprising variety of nutritious and delicious recipes that you can make by using the advantage of hot air. If you like the taste of deep fried foods, this collection of 365 recipes will become your new favorite kitchen companion. Each recipe is tested before making to ensure you are getting the best in quality and flavor.

Most of the recipes call for a nonstick cooking spray. Actually, the manufacturers recommend using high-quality oil sprays for easier cooking. You can also choose your favorite types of fat like olive oil, butter, or coconut oil. Then, you can use misters for frying but just keep in mind – never pour oil into your machine.

This recipe collection is chock-full of great recipes that are written in an easy to follow fashion. The book will guide you every step of the way in order to make all-star recipes that are sure to impress everyone. From rich breakfast frittata to juicy steak and more amazing recipes, you'll surely find the perfect dish for you and your family.

This recipe collection includes breakfast, lunch, dinner, snacks, and even desserts. You will find the recipes that can add some WOW factor to your everyday cooking, as well some really exciting recipes to throw a fantastic party! As we said before, you will be really suppressed what this innovative kitchen appliance can do for you.

Your air fryer is an all-in-one for quick and easy cooking. Once you get to know your air fryer, it opens up a lot of possibilities. Once you learn the basics and become familiar with your air fryer, feel free to experiment and adapt the recipes as you like. A wide range of dishes can be prepared in the air fryer and you can convert a favorite stove-top dish to be air fryer–friendly. It all boils down to versatility, right?

Cooking complete meals to perfection has never been easier. Let this recipe collection prove itself. Enjoy!

BREAKFAST

1. Cheesy Mushroom and Dill Frittata

(Ready in about 30 minutes | Servings 4)

Ingredients

1 shallot, peeled and thinly sliced into rings

2 cloves garlic

4 cups white mushrooms, chopped

2 tablespoons grapeseed oil

6 large-sized eggs

1/8 teaspoon ground black pepper

1/4 teaspoon red pepper flakes, crushed

1/2 teaspoon salt

1/2 teaspoon fresh dill weed, finely minced

1/2 cup cream cheese of choice

Directions

Firstly, sauté the shallot, garlic, and mushrooms in hot grapeseed oil; allow the sautéed mixture to cool.

Meanwhile, preheat the air fryer to 330 degrees F.

Crack the eggs into a mixing dish; beat the eggs along with the black pepper, red pepper, and salt.

Treat the inside of the baking dish with a pan spray. Pour the egg mixture into the baking dish; stir in the sautéed garlic/mushroom mixture. Top with fresh dill; spread cream cheese over your frittata.

Transfer the baking dish to the air fryer cooking basket. Cook about 30 minutes or till a tester comes out dry and clean.

2. Rich Sausage and Egg Breakfast

(Ready in about 25 minutes | Servings 4)

Ingredients

8 chicken sausages

8 slices of bacon

4 medium-sized eggs

Salt and ground black pepper, to taste

8 slices toast

Directions

Firstly, arrange the sausages and bacon in your air fryer; set the temperature to 320 degrees F and allow it to cook for 10 minutes.

Place the eggs in ramekins and season them with salt and pepper. Cook for 10 more at 400 degrees F or until it's done.

Adjust the seasonings and serve with toast. Enjoy!

3. Breakfast Cherry Muffins

(Ready in about 20 minutes | Servings 4)

Ingredients

1/3 cup flour

1/2 teaspoon baking powder

1/2 teaspoon baking soda

1/2 teaspoon freshly grated nutmeg

1/4 teaspoon ground anise star

1/2 teaspoon ground cinnamon

3 tablespoons granulated sugar

A pinch of salt

A pinch of ground cloves

1/2 stick butter, melted

1/3 cup milk

1 whole egg

1/3 cup dried tart cherries

Directions

Preheat your air fryer to 392 degrees F.

Next, sift the flour into a mixing dish and add the baking powder, baking soda, nutmeg, anise star, cinnamon, and granulated sugar. Add the salt and cloves, and mix well.

In another mixing dish, beat the butter, along with the milk and egg; beat well to combine. Throw the butter mixture into the flour mixture. Then add the cherries and mix again.

Scrape the batter into the muffin cups; then, place it in the air fryer basket; set the timer to 15 minutes. Allow your muffins to cool slightly before removing from the muffin cups. Bon appétit!

4. Coconut Challah French Toast

(Ready in about 10 minutes | Servings 2)

Ingredients

2 eggs, beaten

1/4 teaspoon ground allspice

1/2 teaspoon cinnamon

1/8 teaspoon kosher salt

1/4 teaspoon nutmeg, preferably freshly grated

2 tablespoons coconut butter. at room temperature

4 slices of challah bread

Nonstick cooking spray

Maple syrup, to serve

Shaved coconut, to serve

Directions

Start by preheating your air fryer to 356 degrees F.

Then, take a mixing dish and gently beat the eggs, along with the seasonings. Butter both sides of the challah slices. Dip each slice of bread in the spiced egg mixture.

Now, arrange the slices of bread in your air fryer. Then, set the timer for 2 minutes.

After that, pause your air fryer; take out the pan. Treat the bread with a nonstick cooking spray; make sure to spray both sides.

Return your pan to the air fryer and cook another 4 minutes. When the slices of challah are golden brown, you can serve your French toast.

Divide French toast among serving plates and drizzle each portion with maple syrup. Add shaved coconut and serve immediately. Enjoy!

5. The Easiest English Muffin Sandwich Ever

(Ready in about 10 minutes | Servings 1)

Ingredients

1 large-sized egg

Sea salt and ground black pepper, to taste

1/2 teaspoon red pepper flakes, crushed

2 strips of bacon

1 English muffin

1/2 tomato, sliced

Directions

Crack your egg into an ovenproof soufflé cup; sprinkle the salt, black pepper, and red pepper on it.

Place the egg along with the bacon and English muffin in your air fryer.

Turn air fryer to 395 degrees F and set the timer for 6 minutes. Garnish with tomato slices and enjoy!

6. Winter Vegetarian Frittata

(Ready in about 30 minutes | Servings 4)

Ingredients

1 leek, peeled and thinly sliced into rings

2 cloves garlic, finely minced

3 medium-sized carrots, finely chopped

2 tablespoons olive oil

6 large-sized eggs

Sea salt and ground black pepper, to taste

1/2 teaspoon dried marjoram, finely minced

1/2 cup yellow cheese of choice

Directions

Sauté the leek, garlic, and carrot in hot olive oil until they are tender and fragrant; reserve.

In the meantime, preheat your air fryer to 330 degrees F. In a bowl, whisk the eggs along with the salt, ground black pepper, and marjoram.

Then, grease the inside of your baking dish with a nonstick cooking spray. Pour the whisked eggs into the baking dish. Now, stir in the sautéed carrot mixture. Top with the cheese shreds.

Then, place the baking dish in the air fryer cooking basket. Cook about 30 minutes and serve warm.

7. Raisin Bread French Toast

(Ready in about 10 minutes | Servings 2)

Ingredients

2 eggs, beaten

4 tablespoons evaporated milk

1/4 teaspoon ground cinnamon

1/4 teaspoon kosher salt

1/2 teaspoon cardamom

2 tablespoons butter or margarine, softened

4 slices raisin bread

Icing sugar, to serve

Directions

Firstly, preheat your air fryer to 356 degrees F.

Next, whisk the eggs, along with the milk, cinnamon, salt, and cardamom. Butter the bread slices. Soak the bread in the egg mixture. Place the bread slices in your air fryer. Then, set the timer for 2 minutes.

Turn your bread slices and cook on the other side another 2 to 3 minutes.

Divide French toast among serving plates; dust with icing sugar. Garnish with some extra raisins if desired. Enjoy!

8. Turkey Bacon and Colby Rolls

(Ready in about 10 minutes | Servings 4)

Ingredients

8 ounces canned crescent rolls

8 ounces Colby cheese, shredded

1 pound turkey bacon, chopped

Greek style yogurt, to serve

Directions

Start by preheating the air fryer to 330 degrees F.

Cut the dough into "sheets". Combine shredded Colby cheese and bacon. Place the mixture in the middle of each dough sheet.

Create the rolls and transfer them to the cooking basket. Cook for about 7 minutes.

Then, set the timer to 390 degrees F and cook for 2 to 3 minutes longer or until your rolls are golden brown. Serve with Greek yogurt.

9. Blueberry Bread Rolls

(Ready in about 10 minutes | Servings 8)

Ingredients

8 slices of 2-day-old bread

1/4 cup tablespoons Ricotta cheese, softened

1/4 cup blueberries

2 medium-sized eggs

3 tablespoons evaporated milk

1/3 cup sugar

1/2 teaspoon freshly grated nutmeg

1/4 teaspoon ground cinnamon

Directions

Cut the crust from the bread slices; flatten them out with a rolling pin.

Place Ricotta cheese on each slice of bread. Top with the blueberries. Roll each slice of bread up tightly.

In a mixing dish, whisk the eggs and milk. In a separate mixing dish, combine the sugar, nutmeg, and cinnamon.

Dip each roll in the egg/milk mixture; then, roll each one in the seasoned sugar mixture.

Place bread rolls in the air fryer basket. Lightly oil with a nonstick cooking spray. Cook for 5 minutes at 330 degrees F.

10. Spicy Morning Bacon

(Ready in about 10 minutes | Servings 6)

Ingredients

2 tablespoons sugar

1/2 teaspoon red pepper flakes, crushed

1/2 teaspoon allspice

12 slices bacon

Directions

In a mixing bowl, combine the sugar, red pepper, and allspice. Throw in the bacon and stir to coat well.

Lay the bacon slices in the cooking basket.

Cook for about 8 minutes at 350 degrees F; work with batches. Serve with your favorite mustard and enjoy!

11. Tropical Crunchy Granola

(Ready in about 20 minutes | Servings 6)

Ingredients

1 cup rolled oats

1/4 cup pecans, chopped

1/2 cup sliced almonds

3 tablespoons coconut oil, softened

1/8 teaspoon kosher salt

3 tablespoons agave syrup

1/2 teaspoon pure almond extract

1 teaspoon pure vanilla extract

1/2 cup dried pineapple, chopped

1/4 cup dried dates, chopped

1/4 cup raisins

Directions

In a large-sized mixing bowl, stir the oats and nuts. Give it a good stir.

In another mixing bowl, combine the coconut oil, kosher salt, agave syrup, almond extract, and vanilla extract. Pour the coconut oil mixture over the dry oat/nut mixture; stir to combine.

Place the mixture in the air fryer basket. Cook for 8 minutes at 300 degrees. Now, pause your air fryer and stir; continue to cook an additional 8 minutes.

Transfer your granola to a bowl; throw in the fruit. Enjoy your morning!

12. Cheddar Baked Eggs

(Ready in about 15 minutes | Servings 3)

Ingredients

3 tablespoons olive oil

1 tablespoon fresh thyme, finely minced

1 tablespoon fresh parsley, finely minced

2 spring garlic, chopped

1 red onion, chopped

6 tablespoons heavy cream

6 large-sized eggs

1/2 teaspoon fresh or dried dill

1/2 teaspoon salt

1/4 teaspoon ground black pepper

1/2 cup Cheddar cheese shreds

Directions

Take three small ramekins; then, grease them with the oil. Add the thyme, parsley, spring garlic, and red onion.

Place the ramekins in the air fryer basket; cook at 350 degrees for 2 minutes. Now, divide heavy cream among ramekins; crack 2 eggs into each ramekin. Season with the dill, salt and ground black pepper.

Top with Cheddar cheese and return to the cooker. Bake for 8 minutes at 350 degrees F. Taste, adjust the seasonings and serve right away.

13. Baked Cottage Omelet

(Ready in about 10 minutes | Servings 4)

Ingredients

3 eggs, beaten

3 tablespoons frozen kale, thawed and drained

2 tablespoons Cottage cheese

2 tomatoes, sliced

1/4 teaspoon dried thyme

1/4 teaspoon dried basil

Directions

Lightly grease a baking dish with a nonstick cooking spray.

Next, add all ingredients to the baking dish and stir to combine.

Bake for 10 minutes at 330 degrees F.

14. Mediterranean Feta and Prosciutto Rolls

(Ready in about 10 minutes | Servings 4)

Ingredients

8 ounces canned crescent rolls

8 ounces Feta cheese, shredded

1 pound prosciutto, chopped

1/2 cup olives, pitted and sliced

Directions

Firstly, preheat your air fryer to 330 degrees F.

Cut the dough into "sheets". Combine Feta cheese, prosciutto, and olives. Place Feta mixture in the middle of each dough sheet.

Next, create the rolls and transfer them to the cooking basket. Cook for about 7 minutes.

Then, set the timer to 390 degrees F and cook for 2 to 3 minutes longer or until your rolls are golden brown. Serve with tomato ketchup.

15. Plum Fruit Roll-Ups

(Ready in about 15 minutes | Servings 4)

Ingredients

8 slices soft white bread, crustless

2 tablespoons sour cream

6 tablespoons cream cheese, at room temperature

10 plums, pitted and sliced

3 tablespoons evaporated milk

2 eggs

1/4 teaspoon ground cinnamon

1/2 teaspoon ground anise star

1/4 teaspoon vanilla paste

1/3 cup sugar

Directions

Using a rolling pin, flatten bread slices out. Then, mix the sour cream and cream cheese in a bowl.

Place about 1 tablespoon of cream cheese mixture on each bread slice. Top with the plums.

Roll each slice of bread up tightly. Now, in a shallow mixing bowl, thoroughly whisk the milk and egg.

In another mixing bowl, combine the rest of the above ingredients. Dip roll-ups in the egg mixture. Then, roll them in the sugar mixture.

Place prepared rolls in an air fryer basket. Brush them with an oil spray and cook at 330 degrees F for 5 minutes.

16. Walnut and Chocolate Donuts

(Ready in about 15 minutes | Servings 4)

Ingredients

1/2 cup chocolate frosting

1 tablespoon water

1/4 teaspoon ground cinnamon

1/4 teaspoon grated nutmeg

1 can flaky-style biscuit dough

1 cup chocolate frosting

1/2 cup walnuts, chopped

Directions

In a bowl, beat the chocolate frosting and water until creamy and smooth. Now, add the cinnamon and nutmeg and mix again until everything is uniform.

Cut your dough into eight biscuits; now, gently flatten them with a rolling pin. After that, cut a hole (about 1-inch) in the center of each biscuit.

Spritz your biscuits with a nonstick cooking spray. Transfer your biscuits to the cooking basket in a single layer. Working with batches, bake your biscuits for 10 minutes at 330 degrees F.

Next, add the chocolate frosting. Drizzle the reserved chocolate frosting over the top. Top with chopped walnuts.

17. Italian Salami and Cheese Crescent Squares

(Ready in about 10 minutes | Servings 4)

Ingredients

1 can crescent roll, refrigerated

4 large-sized eggs, well beaten

Kosher salt and ground black pepper, to taste

1 tablespoon fresh coriander, minced

2 slices Italian Genoa salami, halved lengthwise

4 slices Provolone cheese

Directions

Firstly, unroll the crescent rolls. Split the dough in order to form 4 rectangles. Fold up the edges of each rectangle.

Lay 1 rectangle in the air fryer basket; now, crack 1 egg into it. Sprinkle with salt, ground black pepper, and coriander.

Add 1 piece of Genoa salami and top with 1 slice of Provolone cheese. Repeat with the remaining rolls.

Bake at 300 degrees F for 10 minutes, or until they're golden brown.

18. Hash Brown Breakfast Casserole

(Ready in about 15 minutes | Servings 4)

Ingredients

6 ounces canned cream of chicken soup

1/2 cup Cottage cheese

Sea salt and ground black pepper, to your liking

1 ½ cups hash brown potatoes, shredded

1/3 cup shallot, chopped

2 cloves garlic, peeled and finely minced

1 tablespoon fresh parsley, finely minced

1 cup yellow cheese, shredded

1/2 cup breadcrumbs

2 tablespoons melted butter

Directions

In a large-sized bowl, whisk the soup, cheese, salt, and ground black pepper. Stir in shredded hash brown potatoes, shallot, garlic, parsley, and cheese. Mix well to combine.

Scrape the mixture evenly into a baking dish.

In a separate bowl, combine together breadcrumbs and melted butter. Sprinkle this mixture evenly on top of potato mixture.

Bake approximately 15 minutes at 300 degrees F. Eat warm, garnished with sour cream and tomato ketchup.

19. Scallion and Fontina Cheese Omelet

(Ready in about 10 minutes | Servings 2)

Ingredients

3 medium-sized eggs, beaten

4 tablespoons scallions, chopped

3 tablespoons Fontina cheese

1 red bell pepper, chopped

1 green bell pepper, chopped

1/2 teaspoon salt

1/4 teaspoon ground black pepper

1 tablespoon fresh basil, chopped

Directions

Spritz a 6-inch baking dish with a nonstick cooking spray.

Add all of the above ingredients to your baking dish; stir until everything is well incorporated.

Bake at 330 degrees F approximately 10 minutes. Serve right away with iceberg lettuce and enjoy!

20. Cheese and Eggs in Brioche Rolls

(Ready in about 10 minutes | Servings 2)

Ingredients

4 brioche rolls

4 tablespoons melted butter

4 slices Swiss cheese, or cheddar

1/2 teaspoon salt

1/4 teaspoon ground black pepper, or to taste

1/2 teaspoon cayenne pepper, or to taste

1/2 teaspoon marjoram

4 eggs

Directions

Cut off the top of each brioche roll; scoop out insides in order to create a shell. The hole should be enough for 1 large egg.

Brush inside with the melted butter. Add 1 slice of Swiss cheese to the inside of each "shell".

Place your brioche shells in a cooking basket; season with salt, black pepper, cayenne pepper, and marjoram.

Crack an egg into each brioche. Bake them about 8 minutes at 330 degrees F. Serve and enjoy!

21. Spicy Pepperoncini Puff Pastry

(Ready in about 10 minutes | Servings 4)

Ingredients

1 can refrigerated crescent roll

4 whole eggs, well beaten

1 tablespoon pepperoncini, finely minced

Kosher salt and ground black pepper, to taste

4 slices Teleme cheese

Directions

Unroll the crescent rolls and make four rectangles. Fold up the edges of each rectangle.

Lower 1 rectangle onto the cooking basket; crack 1 egg into each piece. Sprinkle minced pepperoncini over it. Season with salt and ground black pepper.

Top with Teleme cheese. Repeat with the other pieces. Now, cook in your air fryer for 10 minutes at 300 degrees F or till they're golden brown.

Serve with yogurt and tomato ketchup. Bon appétit!

22. Swiss Hash Brown Casserole

(Ready in about 15 minutes | Servings 4)

Ingredients

1/2 cup cream cheese of choice

6 ounces canned cream of celery soup

1/4 teaspoon ground black pepper, or to your liking

1/4 teaspoon salt

1/4 teaspoon cayenne pepper

1/8 teaspoon freshly grated nutmeg

1 ½ cups hash brown potatoes, shredded

1 red onion, peeled and chopped

2 cloves garlic, peeled and finely minced

1 cup Swiss cheese, grated

1/2 cup breadcrumbs

2 tablespoons butter, melted

1 tablespoon fresh cilantro, finely minced

Directions

In a mixing dish, beat cream cheese along with the soup, black pepper, salt, cayenne pepper, and nutmeg. Stir in potatoes, onion, garlic, and Swiss cheese. Mix until everything is thoroughly combined.

Scrape the mixture into a baking dish.

In another mixing dish, combine the breadcrumbs and butter together. Spread this mixture evenly on top of potato/cheese mixture. Top with fresh cilantro.

Bake at 300 degrees F approximately 15 minutes. Bon appétit!

23. Vegetable and Cottage Cheese Omelet

(Ready in about 10 minutes | Servings 2)

Ingredients

4 medium-sized eggs, beaten

4 tablespoons Cottage cheese

2 tablespoons sour cream

1 bell pepper, seeded and chopped

1/2 cup cherry tomatoes, halved

1/2 teaspoon salt

1/4 teaspoon ground black pepper

1 tablespoon fresh cilantro, chopped

1/2 cup fresh chives, chopped

Directions

Firstly, treat a 6-inch baking dish with a spray coating.

Add all ingredients, except for chives, to the baking dish; give it a good stir.

Bake about 10 minutes at 330 degrees F. Serve garnished with fresh chives. Bon appétit!

24. Mediterranean Puff Pastry Triangles

(Ready in about 10 minutes | Servings 4)

Ingredients

1 can crescent dinner roll, refrigerated

1 tablespoon fresh basil, finely minced

1 teaspoon oregano, dried

3 tablespoons black olives, pitted and finely chopped

Kosher salt and ground black pepper, to taste

1 cup crumbled Feta cheese

Directions

Unroll the crescent rolls and make 4 equal pieces. Do not forget to pat out each piece of dough.

Place 1 piece of dough in a cooking basket. Sprinkle with basil, oregano, black olives, salt and ground black pepper.

Lastly, top with Feta cheese. Fold it and create the triangle. Repeat with the other rolls and bake for 10 minutes at 300 degrees F. Bon appétit!

25. Asparagus and Ham Casserole

(Ready in about 15 minutes | Servings 2)

Ingredients

3 slices of bread

1 egg, beaten

1/2 cup milk

1/2 cup Mozzarella cheese, grated

1/2 teaspoon sea salt

1/2 teaspoon ground black pepper

1/2 teaspoon paprika

1/2 teaspoon dried dill weed

2 slices ham, diced

3 asparagus spears, chopped

Directions

Lightly grease an ovenproof baking dish. Then, remove the crusts from the bread slices; cut them into cubes.

Transfer the bread cubes to the baking dish.

In a mixing bowl, whisk the eggs and milk. Stir in 1/2 of Mozzarella cheese; add the salt, black pepper, paprika, and dill weed. Pour 3/4 egg/cheese mixture over the bread cubes.

Add the ham and top with asparagus spears. Pour the remaining egg/cheese mixture over the top; lastly, add the remaining Mozzarella cheese.

Bake the casserole at 330 degrees F for about 15 minutes. Serve warm.

26. Date and Pineapple Breakfast Muffins

(Ready in about 20 minutes | Servings 4)

Ingredients

1/3 cup flour

1 teaspoon baking powder

1/4 teaspoon ground anise star

1/4 teaspoon ground cloves

1/2 teaspoon ground cinnamon

3 tablespoons sugar

1/8 teaspoon kosher salt

1/2 stick melted butter

1 whole egg

1/3 cup milk

1/4 cup dried pineapple, chopped

1/4 cup dried dates, pitted and chopped

Directions

Preheat your air fryer to 392 degrees F.

In a mixing bowl, combine the flour, baking powder, anise, cloves, cinnamon, sugar, and salt. Mix until everything is well combined.

In another bowl, cream the butter, along with the egg and milk. Add the wet butter/egg mixture to the dry flour mixture. Then add the dried fruits and mix again to combine well.

Scrape the batter into the muffin cups. Bake about 15 minutes. Allow your muffins to cool on a wire rack. Bon appétit!

27. Bacon and Scallion Muffins

(Ready in about 25 minutes | Servings 6)

Ingredients

2 tablespoons vegetable oil

6 slices bacon

1 box corn muffin mix

Salt and ground black pepper, to taste

1 teaspoon marjoram

1/2 teaspoon mustard seeds

1/4 teaspoon celery seeds

4 tablespoons scallions, chopped

1/3 cup Mozzarella cheese, shredded

Directions

Heat the oil in a nonstick skillet over medium-high heat.

Fry the bacon for about 6 minutes. Now, drain the bacon using a paper towel. Chop and reserve.

Prepare the muffin mix according to the manufacturer's directions. Stir in the remaining ingredients along with the bacon bits.

Fill the mini muffin pan with prepared batter. Now, bake your muffins at 330 degrees F for 15 minutes. Serve warm and enjoy!

28. Cheddar Zucchini Cakes

(Ready in about 20 minutes | Servings 4)

Ingredients

1 zucchini, grated

2 tablespoons sea salt

1-2 cloves garlic, finely minced

1/2 cup onion, finely chopped

1 tablespoon fresh dill, finely chopped

1/4 teaspoon freshly cracked black pepper

1 egg, lightly beaten

1/2 cup Cheddar cheese, grated

1/4 cup all-purpose flour

1/4 teaspoon baking powder

Directions

Firstly, in a bowl, toss the zucchini with the salt; allow it to stand for 10 minutes.

Drain and rinse the zucchini. Now, transfer the zucchini to a paper towel and squeeze to remove excess liquid.

Combine the zucchini with the other ingredients. Make the balls using 1 tablespoon of the mixture. Then, gently flatten your balls. Spritz them with a cooking oil.

Bake zucchini cakes in a single layer for 10 minutes at 330 degrees F. Serve with Greek-style yogurt. Enjoy!

29. Honey and Walnut French Toast

(Ready in about 10 minutes | Servings 4)

Ingredients

4 eggs, beaten

A pinch of kosher salt

1/2 teaspoon lemon zest

1/2 teaspoon cinnamon

2 tablespoons coconut butter, softened

8 slices of French bread

Nonstick cooking spray

Honey, to serve

Chopped walnuts, to serve

Directions

Preheat the air fryer to 356 degrees F.

Next step, using a fork, whisk the eggs, along with the salt, lemon zest, and cinnamon; whisk the eggs until foamy.

Butter both sides of the bread slices. Soak bread slices in the egg mixture. Then, place the slices of bread in the air fryer. Let it cook for 2 minutes.

Now, pause the machine; take out the pan. Spritz the bread slices with a cooking spray; make sure to spray on all sides.

Return the pan to the air fryer; cook an additional 4 minutes or until they're golden brown. Garnish with honey and chopped walnuts. Bon appétit!

30. Super Easy Corn Bread

(Ready in about 20 minutes | Servings 6)

Ingredients

3/4 cup all-purpose flour

1 cup cornmeal

1/4 teaspoon kosher salt

1 teaspoon brown sugar

1/2 teaspoon baking soda

1 ½ teaspoons baking powder

2 eggs, lightly whisked

1 ½ cups buttermilk

5 tablespoons melted butter

Directions

Firstly, butter and flour two mini loaf pans.

In a large-sized mixing dish, thoroughly combine the flour, cornmeal, salt, sugar, baking soda, and baking powder. You can use a wire whisk.

In another mixing dish or a measuring cup, mix the eggs with buttermilk and butter. Fold the egg/ buttermilk mixture into the dry flour mixture; stir to combine well.

Spoon the batter into the loaf pans. Bake about 20 minutes at 330 degrees F or until a wooden stick inserted into the middle of your bread comes out dry and clean.

Of course, you can bake in batches as needed. Serve with honey spread, if desired.

31. Pastry with Strawberry Jam

(Ready in about 15 minutes | Servings 4)

Ingredients

1 can crescent dinner rolls, refrigerated

8 tablespoons strawberry jam

1 large-sized egg, whisked

Icing sugar, to serve

Directions

Roll the dough out on a clean surface.

Place 2 tablespoons of the jam in the center of each square; create a triangle. Repeat with the remaining dough.

Brush all triangles with the whisked egg.

Bake at 350 degrees F about 12 minutes or until golden. Transfer them to a serving platter and dust with icing sugar. Bon appétit!

32. Sausage and Eggs with Bell Peppers

(Ready in about 22 minutes | Servings 4)

Ingredients

8 small sausages

1 red bell pepper, seeded and thinly sliced

1 green bell pepper, seeded and thinly sliced

4 medium-sized eggs

1/2 teaspoon sea salt

1/2 teaspoon freshly cracked black pepper

8 slices of toasted bread

Directions

Place the sausages and bell peppers in the air fryer. Cook at 320 degrees F for 10 to 12 minutes.

Crack the eggs into the ramekins; sprinkle them with salt and black pepper. Cook for 10 more minutes at 400 degrees F.

Serve with your favorite toasted bread and enjoy!

33. Hazelnut Bread Pudding

(Ready in about 40 minutes | Servings 6)

Ingredients

8 slices toasted white bread, cubed

2 large-sized eggs, beaten

1 cup milk

1/2 cup buttermilk

1/2 cup half-and-half

1/3 cup honey

1/4 teaspoon pure hazelnut extract

1/2 teaspoon pure vanilla extract

4 tablespoons margarine, at room temperature

3/4 cup sugar

2 tablespoons golden raisin

1/2 cup hazelnuts, chopped

Directions

Place bread cubes in a large-sized bowl.

In a separate mixing bowl, beat the eggs, milk, buttermilk, half-and-half, honey, hazelnut extract, and vanilla extract.

Pour the mixture over bread cubes. Allow bread mixture to sit at least 10 minutes. In another bowl, combine the remaining ingredients.

Now, pour 1/2 of the prepared bread mixture into two loaf pans. Top with 1/2 of hazelnut mixture. Repeat these layers one more time.

Using a wide spoon, press it down to soak bread cubes well. Transfer the pans to the air fryer basket; bake for 30 minutes at 310 degrees F. Serve at room temperature.

34. Raisin and Almond Muffins

(Ready in about 15 minutes | Servings 6)

Ingredients

1/3 cup flour

1 teaspoon baking powder

3 tablespoons granulated sugar

1 teaspoon vanilla essence

1/2 teaspoon almond extract

1/2 teaspoon ground cardamom

1/2 teaspoon ground nutmeg

Pinch of salt

1 egg

1/3 cup milk

1/4 cup butter, melted

1/3 cup raisins

3 tablespoons minced almonds

Directions

Begin by preheating your air fryer to 392 degrees F.

Add the flour to a bowl, along with the baking powder, granulated sugar, vanilla, almond extract, cardamom, nutmeg, and salt. Mix until everything is well combined.

In another mixing bowl, whisk the egg with milk and melted butter. Stir this egg mixture into the dry flour mixture. Now, stir until just moistened.

Then, add the raisins and almonds, and mix again.

Scrape your batter into four muffin cups; carefully transfer them to the air fryer basket.

Next, set the timer to 15 minutes. Let the muffins cool before removing from the cups!

35. Nana's Sweet Corn Bread

(Ready in about 20 minutes | Servings 6)

Ingredients

1 cup cornmeal

3/4 cup all-purpose flour

1/2 teaspoon baking soda

1 ½ teaspoon baking powder

A pinch of salt

1/2 cup sugar

1/2 cup honey

2 eggs, lightly whisked

1/2 cup rice milk

1 cup buttermilk

5 tablespoons melted butter

Directions

Firstly, grease 2 mini loaf pans using a nonstick cooking spray.

In a mixing bowl, combine the cornmeal, flour, baking soda, baking powder, and salt. Now, add the sugar and honey.

In another mixing dish, combine the remaining ingredients until everything is well incorporated. Fold the egg mixture into the flour mixture; give it a good stir.

Scrape the batter into the loaf pans. Now, bake about 20 minutes at 330 degrees F or until a tester inserted into the middle of corn bread comes out dry and clean.

36. Chocolate Puff Pastry

(Ready in about 15 minutes | Servings 4)

Ingredients

1 can crescent dinner rolls, refrigerated

8 tablespoons milk chocolate chips

1 large-sized egg, beaten

Directions

Firstly, roll and flatten crescent dinner rolls on a clean work surface.

Place 2 tablespoons of the milk chocolate chips in the center of each square; fold the dough to make 4 triangles.

Then, brush your triangles with already beaten egg.

Bake at 350 degrees F approximately 12 minutes. Dust with ground cinnamon if desired. Bon appétit!

37. English Muffins with Eggs and Salami

(Ready in about 10 minutes | Servings 2)

Ingredients

2 whole eggs

1/2 teaspoon paprika

Sea salt and ground black pepper, to taste

4 thin slices of salami

2 English muffins

Yellow mustard, of choice

Iceberg lettuce, to garnish

Directions

Crack the eggs into an ovenproof ramekin; sprinkle the paprika, salt, and ground black pepper over them.

Place the eggs along with the slices of salami and English muffin in the air fryer.

Turn air fryer to 395 degrees F; let it cook approximately 6 minutes. Garnish with the mustard and iceberg lettuce leaves. Enjoy!

38. Chocolate and Hazelnut Treat

(Ready in about 10 minutes | Servings 4)

Ingredients

1/2 cup chocolate frosting

1 tablespoon water

1 tablespoon coconut butter, melted

1/4 teaspoon ground cinnamon

1/2 teaspoon vanilla paste

1 can flaky-style biscuit dough

1 cup chocolate frosting

1/2 cup hazelnuts, chopped

Directions

In a mixing bowl, combine the chocolate frosting, water, and coconut butter. Then, mix until creamy and smooth. Add the cinnamon and vanilla paste; mix again.

Cut the dough into 8 biscuits; gently flatten them using a rolling pin. Now, cut a hole (about 1-inch) in the center of each biscuit.

Treat your biscuits with a nonstick cooking spray. Then, transfer them to the cooking basket. Working with batches, bake the biscuits for 10 minutes at 330 degrees F.

Top with chocolate frosting and hazelnuts. Enjoy!

39. Hash Brown Casserole with Mushroom

(Ready in about 20 minutes | Servings 4)

Ingredients

1/2 cup Ricotta cheese

6 ounces canned cream of mushroom soup

1/2 teaspoon salt

1/2 teaspoon cayenne pepper

1/4 teaspoon ground black pepper, or to your liking

1 ½ cups hash brown potatoes, shredded

1 onion, peeled and chopped

2 cloves garlic, peeled and finely minced

1 cup button mushrooms

1 cup Cheddar cheese, shredded

1/2 cup breadcrumbs

2 tablespoons butter, melted

Directions

In a mixing bowl, beat Ricotta cheese along with the cream of mushroom soup, salt, cayenne pepper, and black pepper. Stir in hash brown potatoes, onion, garlic, mushrooms, and cheese. Stir until everything is thoroughly combined.

Spoon this mixture into a baking dish.

In another mixing bowl, combine the breadcrumbs and butter together. Spread this mixture evenly over the top of potato mixture.

Bake at 300 degrees for 15 to 17 minutes. Bon appétit!

40. Chocolate Blackberry Puff Pastry

(Ready in about 15 minutes | Servings 4)

Ingredients

1 can crescent dinner rolls, refrigerated

4 tablespoons dark chocolate, finely chopped

4 tablespoons blackberry jam

1 large-sized egg, beaten

Confectioners' sugar, for dusting

Directions

Using a rolling pin, roll crescent dinner rolls on a clean surface.

Place 2 tablespoons of the dark chocolate and 2 tablespoons of blackberry jam in the center of each square; fold the dough to make 4 triangles.

Now, brush the triangles with already beaten egg.

Bake about 12 minutes at 350 degrees F. Dust with confectioners' sugar and serve. Bon appétit!

41. Spinach and Mushroom Frittata

(Ready in about 30 minutes | Servings 4)

Ingredients

1 cup green onions, finely chopped

2 green garlic, minced

2 tablespoons olive oil

4 cups cremini mushrooms, chopped

6 eggs

1 cup spinach leaves, torn into small pieces

A pinch of kosher salt

1/4 teaspoon ground black pepper, or to taste

6 tablespoons Fontina cheese, grated

Fresh chopped cilantro, for garnish

Directions

Prepare the mushroom sauté by stirring green onions, garlic, and mushrooms in hot olive oil.

In the meantime, preheat the air fryer to 330 degrees F. Crack and beat the eggs into a mixing dish; add the spinach and give it a good stir. Add the salt and ground black pepper.

Coat a baking dish with a thin layer of a nonstick cooking spray. Pour the egg/spinach mixture into the baking dish; now, whisk in the mushroom sauté.

Top with Fontina cheese and transfer the baking dish to the cooking basket. Cook approximately 30 minutes at 330 degrees F. Taste it for doneness and serve warm topped with fresh cilantro.

42. Autumn Pear Fritters

(Ready in about 10 minutes | Servings 4)

Ingredients

2 tablespoons cornstarch

1/2 cup flour

1 teaspoon baking powder

A pinch of salt

1 cup oats

1/2 cup milk

1 egg, lightly beaten

1 tablespoon honey

1/2 teaspoon grated nutmeg

1/4 teaspoon ground cloves

1 ground cinnamon

2 pears, peeled, cored and sliced

Icing sugar, to serve

Directions

In a mixing bowl, combine the cornstarch, flour, baking powder, and salt. Next, ground the oats in a food processor to a coarse powder. Add the oats to the cornstarch mixture.

In another mixing bowl, whisk the milk, egg, and honey. Now, stir in the nutmeg, cloves, and cinnamon; you should have the consistency of pancake batter. Dip each pear slice into the batter, making sure to coat them well.

Now, transfer the pears to the air fryer tray. Cook for 4 minutes at 350 degrees F, working with batches. Dust with icing sugar and serve at room temperature.

43. Turkey Bacon and Spinach Egg Cups

(Ready in about 20 minutes | Servings 4)

Ingredients

1 tablespoon olive oil

2 spring onions, white and green parts finely chopped

1 pound spinach leaves, chopped

4 slices of turkey bacon, coarsely chopped

4 eggs

4 tablespoons buttermilk

1/2 teaspoon sea salt

1/2 teaspoon ground black pepper

1/4 teaspoon dried dill weed

1 teaspoon smoked paprika

Whole meal toast, to serve

Directions

Lightly grease four oven safe ramekins using the olive oil. Now, add chopped spring onions, spinach, and turkey bacon to the ramekins.

Next, crack the eggs into a mixing bowl; whisk them with buttermilk. Season with salt, black pepper, and dill weed; whisk again. Divide the mixture between the ramekins.

Place the ramekins into your air fryer for about 20 minutes at 350 degrees F. Sprinkle smoked paprika over each portion and serve with toast. Enjoy!

44. Skinny Baked Eggs

(Ready in about 20 minutes | Servings 4)

Ingredients

1 tablespoon olive oil

1 white onion, chopped

2 cloves garlic, finely minced

2 bell peppers, chopped

1 cup white mushrooms, chopped

4 whole eggs, beaten

4 egg whites, beaten

1 teaspoon sea salt

1/2 teaspoon ground black pepper

1/4 teaspoon cayenne pepper

Hot sauce, for drizzling

Directions

Heat olive oil in a sauté pan over medium heat; then, sauté the onions and garlic until tender and fragrant. Now, add the peppers and mushrooms and continue sautéing while stirring periodically.

In a mixing dish, thoroughly combine the eggs and egg whites. Stir in the salt, black pepper, and cayenne pepper; whisk until it is well combined.

Then, grease four oven safe ramekins with a nonstick cooking spray. Divide the egg/veggie mixture among the ramekins.

Air-fry approximately 20 minutes at 350 degrees F. Drizzle hot sauce over each portion and serve.

45. Baked Eggs with Sausage and Tomato

(Ready in about 20 minutes | Servings 2)

Ingredients

3 eggs

1/4 cup milk

Sea salt and ground black pepper, to taste

1/2 teaspoon cayenne pepper

Pan spray

2 turkey sausages, cooked and sliced

1 medium-sized tomato, chopped

2 slices of bread, cut into sticks

1/4 cup Cheddar cheese, grated

Directions

Preheat your air fryer to 350 degrees F. In a mixing bowl, whisk the eggs, milk, salt, black pepper, and cayenne pepper.

Lightly grease ramekins with pan oil; divide the egg mixture between ramekins.

Add the sausage, tomato, and bread pieces. Then, top with grated cheese and air-fry for 20 minutes or until it is done. Enjoy!

46. Jalapeño and Bacon Sandwiches

(Ready in about 10 minutes | Servings 2)

Ingredients

2 eggs

1 jalapeño, finely minced

1/2 teaspoon sea salt

1/4 teaspoon black pepper, or to taste

4 bacon slices

2 English muffins

Directions

Take two soufflé cups; crack the egg into each cup. Then, add the jalapeño, sea salt, and black pepper.

Preheat the air fryer to 390 degrees F. Add the bacon and English muffins.

Cook for 6 minutes and serve warm.

47. Ground Pork Omelet

(Ready in about 10 minutes | Servings 2)

Ingredients

2 eggs, whisked

3 ½ ounces ground pork

2 cloves garlic, finely minced

1 onion, chopped

1 salt

1/2 teaspoon cayenne pepper

1/2 teaspoon ground black pepper

Directions

Combine all ingredients in a mixing bowl. Now, spoon the mixture into the air fryer tray.

Preheat the machine to 350 degrees F; set timer for 10 minutes. Serve warm.

48. Scrambled Eggs with Tofu

(Ready in about 15 minutes | Servings 2)

Ingredients

2 eggs

8 ounces soft silken tofu, drained

2 tablespoons butter, melted

1/2 teaspoon coarse salt

1/2 teaspoon red pepper flakes, crushed

1/4 teaspoon freshly cracked black pepper, or to taste

Directions

Whisk the 2 eggs until fluffy. Add the tofu and stir well. Grease a baking tray with the butter.

Pour the egg/tofu mixture into the baking tray. Cook it for 8 minutes at 280 degrees F.

Add the salt, red pepper, and black pepper and stir again. Cook another 2 to 3 minutes. Serve.

49. Cheddar and Potato Patties

(Ready in about 15 minutes | Servings 8)

Ingredients

3 pounds potatoes, peeled and grated

1/4 cup olive oil

2 onions, grated

1 tablespoon sea salt

1/2 teaspoon dried basil

1/2 teaspoon dried oregano

1/2 teaspoon cayenne pepper

3/4 teaspoon ground black pepper

2 cups Cheddar cheese, shredded

Directions

Combine all ingredients in a mixing bowl. Then, make the balls with your hands. Then, flatten them to make the patties.

Then, air-fry your patties approximately 15 minutes at 350 degrees F. Serve warm. Bon appétit!

50. Cranberry Oatmeal Muffins

(Ready in about 15 minutes | Servings 6)

Ingredients

3 ounces butter, melted

1/2 cup powdered sugar

2 eggs, well beaten

1/2 cup flour

3 ½ ounces oats

1/2 teaspoon baking powder

2 tablespoons dried cranberries

Spray oil

Directions

In a mixing bowl, beat together the butter and powdered sugar. Add the eggs and continue to beat until soft peaks form.

In a separate mixing bowl, stir the flour, oats, baking powder, and dried cranberries. Add the oat mixture to the butter/egg mixture. Mix just until moistened.

Then, lightly grease the muffin molds with spray oil. Fill each muffin mold with the batter mixture.

Add the molds to the air fryer tray and cook for 12 minutes at 350 degrees F. Serve with warm milk.

51. Country Fried Bacon

(Ready in about 35 minutes | Servings 4)

Ingredients

1/2 cup milk

3 eggs

1 pound bacon strips

3 cups flour

1/2 teaspoon kosher salt

1/4 teaspoon ground black pepper

1/2 teaspoon red pepper flakes

Directions

In a mixing bowl, whisk the milk with eggs; now, add the bacon strips; soak them in the milk/egg mixture for 30 minutes

Take another mixing bowl and whisk together the remaining ingredients.

Now, toss soaked bacon with the flour mixture; toss to coat well.

Air-fry the bacon for about 4 minutes at 340 degrees F.

52. Kale Scrambled Eggs with Feta

(Ready in about 15 minutes | Servings 2)

Ingredients

4 whole eggs

1 cup cream

Salt and ground black pepper, to your liking

1 tablespoon olive oil

1/4 cup kale, torn into pieces

1/2 cup scallions, chopped

1/2 teaspoon garlic puree

2 Roma tomatoes, chopped

1/2 cup Feta cheese, crumbled

Directions

Crack your eggs into a large-sized mixing bowl; then, add the cream, salt, and ground black pepper.

Then, lightly grease a baking dish with olive oil and tilt it to spread evenly. Spoon the egg mixture into the dish. Add the remaining ingredients.

Next, transfer it to your air fryer. Cook for 10 minutes at 300 degrees F. Stir a few times until the eggs become fluffy. Serve warm.

53. Smoked Tofu and Veggie Omelet

(Ready in about 10 minutes | Servings 2)

Ingredients

4 medium-sized eggs, well-beaten

1/2 cup smoked tofu, crumbled

1 red or orange bell pepper, chopped

1 green bell pepper, chopped

1/2 teaspoon smoked paprika

1/2 teaspoon salt

1/4 teaspoon ground black pepper

1 tablespoon fresh cilantro, chopped

4 small radishes, thinly sliced

Directions

Firstly, brush a baking pan with a spray coating.

Add all ingredients, except for radishes, to the pan; gently stir to combine.

Air-fry at 330 degrees F about 10 minutes. Serve garnished with sliced radishes. Bon appétit!

54. Mediterranean Crescent Squares

(Ready in about 15 minutes | Servings 4)

Ingredients

1 can refrigerated crescent roll

4 medium-sized eggs

Sea salt and ground black pepper, to taste

1 tablespoon fresh rosemary, coarsely chopped

4 small-sized slices turkey ham

4 tablespoons Feta cheese, crumbled

1 tablespoon olive oil

Directions

Firstly, unroll the crescents roll and shape it into four rectangles. Fold up the edges of each rectangle.

Lay 1 rectangle in the air fryer basket; now, crack an egg into the center of the rectangle. Season with salt, black pepper, and rosemary. Place a slice of turkey ham on it.

Top with cheese and repeat with the other ingredients. Lastly, drizzle olive oil over each portion. Bake at 300 degrees for 10 minutes. Bon appétit!

55. Three-Pepper Breakfast Casserole

(Ready in about 15 minutes | Servings 4)

Ingredients

6 ounces canned cream of onion soup

1/2 cup soft cheese

1/4 teaspoon ground black pepper

1/2 teaspoon salt

1/2 teaspoon paprika

1 ½ cups hash brown potatoes, shredded

1/2 cup shallots, finely chopped

1 habanero pepper, seeded and minced

1 red bell pepper, chopped

1 green bell pepper, chopped

1 Serrano pepper, chopped

1 cup Cheddar cheese, shredded

1/2 cup breadcrumbs

2 tablespoons butter, melted

Directions

In a mixing bowl, beat onion soup along with soft cheese and seasonings. Stir in hash brown potatoes, shallots, all peppers, and shredded Cheddar cheese. Stir until it is thoroughly combined.

Spoon this mixture into a baking dish.

In a small bowl, beat the breadcrumbs and butter. Top your casserole with this mixture, making sure to spread it evenly. Bake at 300 degrees about 15 minutes. Bon appétit!

56. Breakfast Pumpkin Muffins

(Ready in about 15 minutes | Servings 4)

Ingredients

3 ounces butter, melted

1/2 cup powdered sugar

2 eggs, well beaten

1 cup pumpkin puree

2 tablespoons unsweetened applesauce

1/2 cup flour

3 ½ ounces oats

1/2 teaspoon baking powder

1/2 teaspoon powdered ginger

1 teaspoon vanilla extract

Directions

In a mixing dish, beat together the butter and sugar. Fold in the eggs, pumpkin puree, and applesauce; beat well to combine.

In a separate mixing bowl, combine other ingredients. Add this mixture to the butter mixture and mix just until moistened.

Next step, grease the muffin molds with a spray oil. Fill each muffin mold with the batter.

Transfer the molds to the air fryer; cook at 350 degrees F for 11 to 13 minutes. Enjoy!

57. Two-Mushroom Frittata

(Ready in about 10 minutes | Servings 4)

Ingredients

Nonstick cooking spray

4 eggs, lightly beaten

1/2 cup cremini mushrooms, thinly sliced

1/2 cup porcini mushrooms, thinly sliced

2 cloves garlic, finely minced

2 tablespoons crumbled goat cheese

6 cherry tomatoes, quartered

1/4 teaspoon dried oregano

1/4 teaspoon dried basil

1/2 teaspoon dried rosemary

Chopped fresh chives, to garnish

Directions

Lightly grease a baking dish with a cooking spray. Throw in all ingredients, except chives.

Bake at 330 degrees for 10 minutes. Serve topped with fresh chives. Enjoy!

58. Light and Easy Arugula Scramble

(Ready in about 15 minutes | Servings 2)

Ingredients

4 whole eggs

1/2 cup Ricotta cheese

1/2 cup buttermilk

1/2 teaspoon cayenne pepper

1/4 teaspoon dried oregano

Salt and ground black pepper, to your liking

1 tablespoon olive oil

1 cup arugula, torn into pieces

1/2 teaspoon garlic puree

Directions

Crack the eggs into a mixing dish; then, add the cheese, buttermilk, cayenne pepper, oregano, salt, and black pepper.

Next, brush a baking dish with the olive oil. Spoon the egg mixture into the dish. Cook for 8 minutes at 300 degrees F.

Then, toss in arugula and stir so that it wilts down slightly. Add garlic puree and stir 2 more minutes. Bon appétit!

59. Festive Vegetarian Mushroom Casserole

(Ready in about 15 minutes | Servings 6)

Ingredients

6 ounces canned cream of mushroom soup

1/2 cup cream cheese

2 tablespoons buttermilk

Kosher salt and ground black pepper, to taste

1/2 teaspoon cayenne pepper

1/4 teaspoon dried thyme

1/2 teaspoon dried marjoram

1 ½ cups hash brown potatoes, shredded

2 cloves garlic, peeled and minced

1/2 cup scallions, finely chopped

1 cup cremini mushrooms, thinly sliced

1/2 cup porcini mushrooms, thinly sliced

1 cup Fontina cheese, shredded

2 tablespoons ghee, at room temperature

1/2 cup breadcrumbs

Directions

In a mixing dish, thoroughly combine the soup with cream cheese, buttermilk, and all seasonings.

Stir in hash browns, garlic, scallions, mushrooms, and Fontina cheese. Stir to combine well. Then, scrape the mixture into a baking dish.

In a mixing bowl, beat the ghee and breadcrumbs until well combined. Top your casserole with ghee mixture. Bake at 300 degrees about 15 minutes. Bon appétit!

60. One-More-Bite Cheesy Ham Croquettes

(Ready in about 10 minutes | Servings 6)

Ingredients

For the Filling:

1 pound Monterey Jack cheese, sliced

1 pound ham slices

For the Coating:

1/2 cup seasoned breadcrumbs

1 tablespoon melted butter

1 cup all-purpose flour

2 eggs, well-beaten

Directions

Firstly, wrap ham slices around cheese slices, covering completely. Then, transfer them to the freezer for 10 minutes

Mix breadcrumbs with the melted butter in a shallow dish.

Dredge each croquette in the flour. Then, place them in the beaten eggs. Now, place them in the breadcrumb mixture.

Cook your croquettes in the air fryer for 8 minutes at 350 degrees F. Bon appétit!

61. Decadent Vanilla-Glazed Morning Biscuits

(Ready in about 15 minutes | Servings 6)

Ingredients

1 can flaky-style biscuit dough

1/2 stick butter, melted

1/2 teaspoon cinnamon powdered

1/4 teaspoon ground anise star

1 ½ cups powdered sugar

1 tablespoon pure vanilla extract

2 tablespoons plain milk

Directions

Divide the dough and shape it into eight biscuits. Then, cut a hole in the center of each biscuit.

Then, combine the butter, cinnamon, and anise. Dip each biscuit in the butter mixture; arrange them on a baking pan.

Bake them in an air fryer basket at 330 degrees F for about 12 minutes; work with batches. Transfer them to a cooling rack.

In a medium-sized bowl, combine powdered sugar, vanilla extract, and milk. Dip each biscuit halfway into the glaze. Serve and enjoy.

62. Scrambled Eggs with Smoked Salmon

(Ready in about 15 minutes | Servings 4)

Ingredients

1 tablespoon olive oil

1/2 cup smoked salmon, chopped

1/2 cup spring onions, chopped

4 eggs, lightly beaten

2 tablespoons cream cheese

1 tablespoon milk

Salt and ground black pepper, to taste

1 teaspoon fresh rosemary leaves, minced

1 teaspoon fresh basil leaves, minced

Sage leaves, to garnish

Directions

Grease 4 oven safe ramekins with olive oil. Then, divide smoked salmon and spring onions among oiled ramekins.

Crack an egg into each ramekin, add the cheese, milk, salt, black pepper, rosemary and basil. Now, air-fry it approximately 15 minutes at 350 degrees F.

Garnish with sage leaves and serve warm.

63. Baked Eggs with Roasted Tomatoes

(Ready in about 30 minutes | Servings 4)

Ingredients

1 cup grape tomatoes

1 tablespoon extra-virgin olive oil

1/2 teaspoon coarse salt

1/2 teaspoon freshly ground black pepper, or to your liking

4 eggs

2 tablespoons sour cream

1 sprig rosemary, crushed

3/4 teaspoon dried oregano

Directions

Place the tomatoes in the baking pan. Drizzle olive oil over them; sprinkle with salt, and ground black pepper.

Roast grape tomatoes at 400 degrees F for about 15 minutes, or till they begin to soften. Divide the roasted tomatoes among four oven safe ramekins.

Throw in the remaining ingredients. Now, air-fry it approximately 15 minutes at 350 degrees F. Let your eggs cool slightly before serving. Enjoy!

64. Eggs and Salmon in Brioche

(Ready in about 10 minutes | Servings 4)

Ingredients

4 brioche rolls

4 tablespoons olive oil

1 teaspoon dried rosemary

1 teaspoon dried thyme

4 tablespoons soft cheese

1/2 cup smoked salmon, chopped

3 eggs

Salt and black pepper, to taste

Directions

Cut off the top of each brioche; then, scoop out insides in order to make "shells".

Brush the insides of your "shells" with olive oil. Add the rosemary, thyme and soft cheese to the inside of each brioche shell.

Lay prepared brioche shells in the cooking basket; add the salmon. Crack an egg into each brioche shell; season with salt and black pepper. Bake for 9 minutes at 330 degrees F. Bon appétit!

65. Chorizo and Emmental Frittata

(Ready in about 15 minutes | Servings 4)

Ingredients

1 tablespoon butter, melted

1/2 cup chorizo, chopped

1 bell pepper, chopped

4 eggs

2 tablespoons buttermilk

Salt and ground black pepper, to taste

1 tablespoon fresh thyme leaves, minced

1/2 cup Emmental cheese, shredded

Directions

Butter four oven safe ramekins. Then, divide chorizo and bell pepper among your ramekins.

Crack an egg into each ramekin, add buttermilk, salt, black pepper, and thyme. Now, air-fry approximately 15 minutes at 350 degrees F.

Top with shredded cheese and serve warm.

66. Pecan and Apricot Granola

(Ready in about 15 minutes | Servings 8)

Ingredients

1 cup rolled oats

4 tablespoons sesame seeds

1/4 cup unsweetened coconut, shredded

1/2 cup pecans

2 tablespoons ghee

A pinch of salt

3 tablespoons honey

1/2 teaspoon ground cloves

1/2 teaspoon ground cinnamon

1 cup dried apricots, coarsely chopped

Directions

In a mixing bowl, combine the oats, sesame seeds, coconut, and pecans. Mix well to combine.

In a separate mixing bowl, combine the ghee, salt, honey, cloves, and cinnamon. Pour this mixture into the dry oat mixture; stirring again.

Spoon the mixture into the air fryer basket. Bake at 300 degrees for 15 minutes, stirring once. Allow your granola to cool completely.

Throw in dried apricots and stir to combine. You can freeze this granola for extended storage.

67. Melt-in-Your-Mouth Raspberry Rolls

(Ready in about 10 minutes | Servings 4)

Ingredients

10 slices stale Italian bread, crustless

1/2 cup cream cheese, at room temperature

1/3 cup raspberry jam

2 medium-sized eggs

3 tablespoons evaporated milk

1/3 cup sugar

1/2 teaspoon ground cloves

1 teaspoon pure vanilla extract

1/2 teaspoon pure orange extract

Directions

Firstly, using a rolling pin, flatten each bread slice.

Then, spread cream cheese over each slice of bread. Top with the raspberry jam. Roll each slice of bread up tightly.

In a measuring cup, whisk the eggs and milk. In another mixing dish, combine the remaining ingredients.

Dip each roll in the egg mixture; then, roll each one in the seasoned sugar mixture.

Arrange bread rolls in the air fryer basket. Cook at 330 degrees F for 5 minutes. Work with batches. Enjoy!

68. Tarragon Scrambled Eggs to Go

(Ready in about 10 minutes | Servings 4)

Ingredients

4 eggs, beaten

2 tablespoons tofu cheese, crumbled

1 tablespoon fresh tarragon, chopped

2 tomatoes, sliced

2 tablespoons freshly snipped chives

2 whole-wheat pita pockets

Tomato salsa, to serve

Directions

Lightly grease a baking dish using a nonstick cooking spray.

Throw the eggs, tofu, tarragon, tomatoes, and chives into the baking dish; give it a good stir.

Air-fry for 10 minutes at 330 degrees F. Divide the mixture among two pita pockets and garnish with salsa. Bon appétit!

69. Cheese and Onion Rolls

(Ready in about 15 minutes | Servings 4)

Ingredients

1 (8-ounce) can crescent rolls

1 cup Mainland mild blend, grated

1 yellow onion, sliced

Directions

Start by preheating your air fryer to 330 degrees F. Cut the dough into "sheets".

In a mixing bowl, combine the cheese and onion. Then, spread a small amount of mixture over sheets of dough; then roll them up.

Transfer them to the food basket. Cook for about 8 minutes. Now, increase the temperature to 390 degrees F. Continue cooking for 3 more minutes. Bon appétit!

70. Sunday Pizza Rolls

(Ready in about 10 minutes | Servings 5)

Ingredients

10 slices white bread, crusts removed

1/2 cup soft cheese, at room temperature

1/2 cup tomato ketchup

4 slices ham, chopped

2 medium-sized eggs

4 tablespoons unsweetened evaporated milk

1 packet French onion soup mix

1/2 teaspoon dried oregano

1/2 teaspoon dried basil

Directions

Flatten each bread slice using a rolling pin.

Then, spread soft cheese on each slice of bread. Then, add the ketchup. Top with the ham. Roll each slice of bread up tightly.

In a mixing dish, whisk the eggs, milk, and onion soup mix. Dip each roll in the egg mixture; sprinkle the oregano and basil over all rolls.

Arrange bread rolls in the air fryer basket. Cook at 330 degrees F for 5 to 7 minutes, working with batches. Bon appétit!

71. Asiago and Ham English Muffin

(Ready in about 10 minutes | Servings 1)

Ingredients

1 egg

Salt and ground black pepper, to taste

1/4 teaspoon smoked paprika

2 slices deli-sliced ham

1 slice asiago cheese

1 English muffin

Directions

Crack the egg into an ovenproof soufflé cup. Then, add the salt, black pepper, and smoked paprika. Beat until it is well combined.

Air-fry at 395 degrees Fahrenheit for 6 minutes

Assemble sandwich with baked egg, ham, cheese, and English muffin. Enjoy!

72. Cornbread with Onions and Kalamata Olives

(Ready in about 20 minutes | Servings 6)

Ingredients

1 box prepared cornbread mix

1 ½ teaspoons baking powder

1 teaspoon sugar

1/2 teaspoon sea salt

2 eggs, lightly whisked

1 tablespoon fresh rosemary, roughly chopped

1 cup milk

5 tablespoons melted butter

1/4 cup green onion, thinly sliced

1/2 cup Kalamata olives, pitted and chopped

Directions

Grease 2 mini loaf pans using a nonstick cooking spray.

In a bowl, combine cornbread mix with baking powder, sugar, and salt.

In another mixing bowl, combine the eggs, rosemary, milk, and butter. Fold the egg mixture into the flour mixture; add the onions and olives and stir to combine.

Scrape the batter into the loaf pans. Bake your cornbread about 20 minutes at 330 degrees F or until a wooden stick inserted into the middle of cornbread comes out dry.

73. Favorite Coconut Banana Fritters

(Ready in about 10 minutes | Servings 4)

Ingredients

1/2 cup flour

2 tablespoons cornstarch

1/2 teaspoon baking powder

1/2 teaspoon baking soda

1 cup oats, ground

A pinch of salt

1 egg, lightly beaten

1/2 cup buttermilk

1 tablespoon sugar

1/4 teaspoon ground cloves

1/2 teaspoon ground cinnamon

2 bananas, peeled and sliced

1/2 cup coconut flakes

Confectioners' sugar, to serve

Directions

In a mixing bowl, combine the flour, cornstarch, baking powder, baking soda, oats, and salt.

In another mixing bowl, whisk the egg, buttermilk, sugar, cloves, and cinnamon. Whisk until you have the consistency of pancake batter. Dip each banana slice in the batter, making sure to coat them well.

Air fry them for 4 minutes at 350 degrees F, working in batches. Dust with coconut and confectioners' sugar and serve at room temperature.

LUNCH

74. Stuffed Chicken Breasts

(Ready in about 25 minutes | Servings 2)

Ingredients

1 chicken breast, halved

1 cup soft cheese

1 teaspoon shallot powder

1/2 teaspoon granulated garlic

1 teaspoon fresh or dried parsley

1 egg, beaten

Salt and ground black pepper, to taste

Breadcrumbs

Directions

Firstly, flatten out the chicken breast using a rolling pin.

In a mixing dish, combine the soft cheese with the shallot powder, garlic and parsley.

Place the mixture in the middle of the chicken breasts. Repeat with the remaining half of the chicken breast.

In a shallow bowl, whisk the egg. In another shallow dish, combine the salt, pepper, and breadcrumbs. Dip the chicken breasts in the whisked egg and roll them in the breadcrumbs. Transfer prepared breasts to the air fryer.

Cook at 350 degrees F for 25 minutes. Serve warm.

75. Country-Style Bubble & Squeak

(Ready in about 25 minutes | Servings 4)

Ingredients

Leftover vegetables (stuffing, mash, cabbage, etc.)

1 leek, thinly sliced

2 cloves garlic, finely minced

2 eggs, whisked

1/2 cup yellow cheese, grated

1 cup minced meat

1 teaspoon thyme

3/4 teaspoon sea salt

1/2 teaspoon ground black pepper

Directions

Place your leftover vegetables in a mixing dish.

Add all remaining ingredients and mix to combine; use your hands or wide spatula, it's up to you.

Spoon the mixture into a baking dish. Preheat your air fryer to 350 degrees F. Cook for about 25 minutes or until it's bubbling. Bon appétit!

76. Crispy Paprika Fish Fillets

(Ready in about 15 minutes | Servings 4)

Ingredients

1/2 cup seasoned breadcrumbs

1 tablespoon balsamic vinegar

1/2 teaspoon seasoned salt

1 teaspoon paprika

1/2 teaspoon ground black pepper

1 teaspoon celery seed

2 fish fillets, halved

1 egg, beaten

Directions

Add the breadcrumbs, vinegar, salt, paprika, ground black pepper, and celery seeds to your food processor. Process for about 30 seconds.

Coat the fish fillets with the beaten egg; then, coat them with the breadcrumbs mixture.

Cook at 350 degrees F for about 15 minutes. Bon appétit!

77. Mom's Chicken Wrapped in Bacon

(Ready in about 20 minutes | Servings 6)

Ingredients

6 rashers bacon

1/4 cup cream cheese

1 chicken breast, chop into six pieces

1 teaspoon garlic powder

1/2 teaspoon kosher salt

1/4 teaspoon freshly ground black pepper

Fresh parsley, to serve

Directions

Firstly, spread the bacon rashes with a thin layer of cream cheese.

Place the chicken on top; season with garlic powder, salt and ground black pepper; now, roll them up. You can secure the rolls with toothpicks.

Place the rolls in the air fryer. Cook at 350 degrees F for 15 minutes. Sprinkle chopped fresh parsley over all and serve.

78. Cheesy Au Gratin Potatoes

(Ready in about 20 minutes | Servings 2)

Ingredients

2 large-sized waxy potatoes, sliced

2 eggs, well-beaten

3/4 cup thickened cream

1 tablespoon flour

1/2 teaspoon pink Himalayan salt flakes

Paprika, to taste

1/4 cup fresh parsley, chopped

1/2 cup Colby cheese, grated

Directions

Place the potato slices in the food basket and air-fry them for 10 minutes at 350 degrees F.

To make the topping, combine the eggs, cream, flour, salt, and paprika. Take the potatoes out of your air fryer.

Cover with the topping mixture, sprinkle with the parsley and cheese; increase the temperature to 400 degrees F and cook for a further 10 minutes. Enjoy!

79. Old Bay Shrimp

(Ready in about 10 minutes | Servings 4)

Ingredients

1 ¼ pounds shrimp, shelled and deveined

1/4 teaspoon freshly cracked black pepper

1/2 teaspoon old bay seasoning

1 tablespoon fresh parsley, chopped

1/2 teaspoon salt

1 tablespoon extra-virgin olive oil

Thin slices of lemon, to serve

Directions

Begin by preheating your air fryer to 390 degrees F.

In a mixing dish, thoroughly combine all ingredients, except for lemon slices; toss until everything is well coated.

Transfer the shrimp mixture to the cooking basket; cook about 5 minutes. Taste for doneness and serve right away with thin lemon slices.

80. The Easiest Jacket Potatoes Ever

(Ready in about 15 minutes | Servings 4)

Ingredients

4 medium potatoes

2 tablespoons butter

1/2 cup cream cheese

1 heaped teaspoon capers

1/4 cup Cheddar cheese, grated

1/4 teaspoon red pepper flakes, crushed

1/2 teaspoon sea salt

1/2 teaspoon ground black pepper, or to your liking

Directions

Prick the potatoes with a fork so that they can breathe. Place them in the air fryer for 15 minutes at 350 degrees F.

In the meantime, prepare the filling. Mix all ingredients, except for butter. When the potatoes are cooked, spread them with butter followed by the prepared filling. Serve warm.

81. Delicious Ground Pork Kebabs

(Ready in about 20 minutes | Servings 4)

Ingredients

1 ½ cups pork, minced

2 cloves garlic, peeled and minced

1 red onion, peeled and chopped

1 tablespoon tomato puree

4 tablespoons breadcrumbs

1/2 teaspoon red pepper flakes, crushed

1/2 teaspoon salt

1/2 teaspoon ground black pepper, or to taste

Directions

Combine all ingredients in a mixing bowl. Mix to combine well and form it into sausage shapes.

Cook in your air fryer for 20 minutes at 350 degrees F. Serve over cooked rice.

82. Crispy Catfish Fillets

(Ready in about 20 minutes | Servings 4)

Ingredients

2 catfish fillets

1/2 cup tortilla chips

Juice and rind of 1 lime

1/2 teaspoon garlic powder

1 tablespoon parsley

1/2 teaspoon salt

1/2 teaspoon ground black pepper

1 egg, beaten

Directions

Cut the fillets in half to make 4 pieces. Add tortilla chips, lime, garlic powder, parsley, salt, and ground black pepper to your food processor. Process for about 30 seconds.

Coat the fish with the beaten egg; then, coat them with the tortilla chips mixture.

Let it cook for 15 minutes at 350 degrees F. Bon appétit!

83. Ranchero Beef and Pork

(Ready in about 20 minutes | Servings 4)

Ingredients

1 cup pork, minced

1/2 cup beef, minced

1 cup scallions, peeled and chopped

1 jalapeño pepper, finely minced

1 tablespoon tomato puree

4 tablespoons finely crushed ranch-flavored tortilla chips

1/2 teaspoon salt

1/2 teaspoon ground black pepper, or to taste

1 teaspoon cayenne pepper

Directions

Thoroughly combine all ingredients in a mixing dish. Then, form the mixture into the sausage shapes.

Cook at 350 degrees F for 20 minutes using your air fryer. Serve with boiled potatoes. Enjoy!

84. Cilantro-Basil Spiced Shrimp

(Ready in about 10 minutes | Servings 4)

Ingredients

1 ¼ pounds shrimp, shelled and deveined

2 cloves garlic, minced

1 teaspoon ginger, freshly grated

1/4 teaspoon freshly cracked black pepper

1/2 teaspoon sea salt

1/2 teaspoon crushed red pepper flakes

1 tablespoon fresh cilantro, chopped

1 tablespoon fresh basil leaves, chopped

1 tablespoon extra-virgin olive oil

Directions

Begin by preheating your air fryer to 390 degrees F.

In a mixing dish, combine all ingredients; toss until everything is well combined.

Transfer the shrimp mixture to the cooking basket; cook about 5 minutes. Serve with cooked angel hair pasta.

85. Bubble and Squeak with Turkey

(Ready in about 30 minutes | Servings 4)

Ingredients

Leftover veggie bake

1 onion, thinly sliced

2 eggs, whisked

1/2 teaspoon honey Dijon mustard

1/2 cup Mozzarella cheese, grated

1/2 turkey breast, chopped

1 teaspoon marjoram

3/4 teaspoon sea salt

1/2 teaspoon ground black pepper

Directions

Place your leftover veggie bake in a mixing bowl; mix well to combine.

Next, stir in the onion, eggs, mustard, and Mozzarella cheese. Add the turkey breasts and mix everything with your hands.

Add the other seasonings and mix again. Put the mixture into ramekins; transfer it to the air fryer. Cook at 350 degrees F for 25 minutes, or until it's bubbling. Bon appétit!

86. Parmesan Tilapia Fillets

(Ready in about 20 minutes | Servings 4)

Ingredients

3/4 cup Parmesan cheese, grated

1 tablespoon fresh lemon juice

1/2 teaspoon ground black pepper

1/4 teaspoon crushed red pepper flakes

1/2 teaspoon seasoned salt

1 heaping tablespoon fresh parsley, finely minced

4 small-sized tilapia fillets, halved

2 tablespoons extra-virgin olive oil

Directions

In a large-sized shallow bowl, place Parmesan cheese, followed by lemon juice and all seasonings.

Coat your fillets with olive oil; now, press them into the Parmesan cheese mixture.

Cook at 350 degrees F for about 15 minutes. Enjoy!

87. Garlicky Cilantro Shrimp

(Ready in about 10 minutes | Servings 4)

Ingredients

1 pound shrimp, shelled and deveined

4 cloves garlic, finely minced

1 teaspoon freshly cracked black pepper

1/2 teaspoon sea salt

1 heaping tablespoon fresh cilantro, chopped

2 tablespoons olive oil

Directions

In a mixing dish, combine all of the above ingredients; gently stir until everything is thoroughly combined and shrimp is well coated.

Add your mixture to the cooking basket; cook approximately 5 minutes at 390 degrees F. Serve with cooked corn and enjoy!

88. Grilled Soy Salmon Fillets

(Ready in about 2 hours 10 minutes | Servings 4)

Ingredients

4 salmon fillets

1/4 teaspoon ground black pepper

1/2 teaspoon cayenne pepper

1/2 teaspoon salt

1 teaspoon onion powder

1 tablespoon fresh lemon juice

1/2 cup soy sauce

1/2 cup water

1 tablespoon honey

2 tablespoons extra-virgin olive oil

Directions

Firstly, pat the salmon fillets dry using kitchen towels. Season the salmon with black pepper, cayenne pepper, salt, and onion powder.

To make the marinade, combine together the lemon juice, soy sauce, water, honey, and olive oil. Marinate the salmon for at least 2 hours in your refrigerator.

Arrange the fish fillets on a grill basket in your air fryer. Bake at 330 degrees for 8 to 9 minutes, or until salmon fillets are easily flaked with a fork.

Work with batches and serve warm. Bon appétit!

89. Baked Saucy Lemon Chicken

(Ready in about 30 minutes | Servings 8)

Ingredients

1/4 cup olive oil

4 cloves garlic, minced

1/4 cup dry white wine

Juice of 1 freshly squeezed lemon

1 teaspoon dried basil

1 teaspoon fresh thyme leaves, minced

1/2 teaspoon seasoned salt

1/2 teaspoon freshly cracked black pepper

4 boneless chicken breasts, cut into small pieces

1 lemon, cut into wedges

Directions

Warm the oil in a saucepan over medium-low heat. Then, sauté the garlic for just 1 minute, or until fragrant.

Remove the garlic from the heat; pour in the white wine and lemon juice. Now, add the basil, thyme, salt, and black pepper. Pour the mixture into a baking dish.

Throw in the chicken breasts. Tuck the lemon wedges among the pieces of chicken.

Bake for 30 minutes at 330 degrees F. Serve warm and enjoy!

90. Soy and Ginger Shrimp

(Ready in about 1 hour 10 minutes | Servings 4)

Ingredients

2 tablespoons olive oil

2 tablespoons scallions, finely chopped

2 cloves garlic, chopped

1 teaspoon fresh ginger, grated

1 tablespoon dry white wine

1 tablespoon balsamic vinegar

1/4 cup soy sauce

1 tablespoon sugar

1 pound shrimp

Salt and ground black pepper, to taste

Directions

To make the marinade, warm the oil in a saucepan; cook all ingredients, except the shrimp, salt, and black pepper. Now, let it cool.

Marinate the shrimp, covered, at least an hour, in the refrigerator.

After that, bake the shrimp at 350 degrees F for 8 to 10 minutes (depending on the size), turning once or twice. Season prepared shrimp with salt and black pepper and serve right away!

91. Easy Wilted Spinach with Bacon

(Ready in about 10 minutes | Servings 4)

Ingredients

1 tablespoon canola oil

1 leek, sliced thinly

2 garlic cloves, finely minced

4 slices bacon

6 ounces spinach

Directions

Preheat your air fryer to 340 degrees F.

Add the oil, leeks, garlic, and bacon, and cook for 3 minutes.

Next, pause the machine; add the spinach and cook for another 4 minutes. Serve warm.

92. Stuffed Baked Potatoes

(Ready in about 20 minutes | Servings 4)

Ingredients

2 tablespoons butter

1 tablespoon all-purpose flour

1/2 teaspoon sea salt

1/2 teaspoon ground black pepper

1/2 cup milk

1/2 cup Cheddar cheese

For the Filling:

1/2 pound ground meat

1/2 cup onion, finely chopped

2 cloves garlic, minced

1/4 teaspoon ground black pepper

1/2 teaspoon salt

1/8 cup tomato ketchup

4 potatoes, baked and cooled

Directions

To prepare the sauce, melt the butter in a small-sized pan. Stir in the flour; cook, stirring constantly, for 1 minute.

Add the salt, pepper, and milk. When your sauce has thickened, remove from the heat; now, fold in the cheese and stir until it is completely melted.

Then, prepare the filling. In a nonstick sauté pan, brown the meat, along with the onion and garlic. Stir in the pepper, salt, tomato ketchup; fold in the cheese sauce and stir to combine.

Scoop out the flesh from each potato, creating a shell. Chop potato flesh into small pieces.

Mix the potato flesh with the meat mixture. Fill each potato shell with the mixture. Bake for 15 to 18 minutes at 330 degrees F.

93. Perfect Pork Chops

(Ready in about 20 minutes | Servings 4)

Ingredients

4 center-cut loin pork chops

1 tablespoon fresh thyme, minced

1 tablespoon apple cider vinegar

1 tablespoon whole grain mustard

Salt and ground black pepper, to taste

Directions

Add all ingredients to a mixing bowl. Toss to coat.

Next, add the pork chops to the air fryer basket. Bake for 20 minutes at 400 degrees F, turning once. Serve with your favorite salad.

94. Potatoes with Peppers and Bacon

(Ready in about 15 minutes | Servings 4)

Ingredients

4 potatoes, peeled and cubed

1 red bell pepper, chopped

1 green bell pepper, chopped

5 rashers smoked bacon, diced

1/2 teaspoon sea salt

1 tablespoon melted butter

1 teaspoon cayenne pepper

1/4 teaspoon ground black pepper

1/2 teaspoon garlic powder

1/2 teaspoon onion powder

Directions

Add the potatoes to the cooking basket. Add the pepper, and cook at 360 degrees F for 11 minutes.

Toss in the bacon and cook for 3 additional minutes. Now, add the butter and all seasonings. Serve and enjoy!

95. Warming Winter Beef with Celery

(Ready in about 15 minutes | Servings 4)

Ingredients

9 ounces tender beef, chopped

1/2 cup leeks, chopped

1/2 cup celery stalks, chopped

2 cloves garlic, smashed

2 tablespoons red cooking wine

3/4 cup cream of celery soup

2 sprigs rosemary, chopped

1/4 teaspoon smoked paprika

3/4 teaspoons salt

1/4 teaspoon black pepper, or to taste

Directions

Add the beef, leeks, celery, and garlic to the baking dish; cook for about 5 minutes at 390 degrees F.

Once the meat is starting to tender, pour in the wine and soup. Season with rosemary, smoked paprika, salt, and black pepper. Now, cook an additional 7 minutes. Bon appétit!

96. Italian Sausage with Potatoes

(Ready in about 35 minutes | Servings 4)

Ingredients

1 pound potatoes, cut into bite-sized chunks

1 shallot, cut into wedges

1 bell pepper, cut into strips

2 sprigs thyme

2 sprigs rosemary

Salt and ground black pepper, to your liking

1 tablespoon extra-virgin olive oil

1 pound Italian sausage

Directions

Arrange the potatoes, shallot wedges, and bell peppers on the bottom of the air fryer tray. Sprinkle with the thyme, rosemary, salt, and black pepper.

Next step, place the sausage on top of the vegetables.

Roast for 30 to 35 minutes at 370 degrees, stirring once or twice. Taste your potatoes for doneness and serve warm.

97. Crispy Pan-Fried Beans

(Ready in about 10 minutes | Servings 4)

Ingredients

1/2 cup flour

1 teaspoon garlic, minced

1 teaspoon Garam masala

1/2 cup breadcrumbs

1 tablespoon shallot powder

Salt and crushed red pepper flakes, to taste

10 ounces beans

2 eggs

1 tablespoon olive oil

1 bay leaf

Directions

Mix the flour, garlic, and Garam masala in a bowl; mix well to combine. In another shallow bowl, mix the breadcrumbs with the shallot powder, salt, and red pepper.

Beat the eggs in the third bowl. Now, coat the beans with the flour/garlic mixture. Next, dip them in the beaten egg; lastly, toss the beans in the breadcrumb mixture.

Transfer the beans to the air fryer baking pan; add the oil and bay leaf; cook for 4 minutes at 350 degrees F. Discard the bay leaf and serve warm.

98. Sweet and Spicy Salmon Steak

(Ready in about 2 hours 10 minutes | Servings 2)

Ingredients

2 salmon fillets

1/4 teaspoon ground black pepper

1/2 teaspoon kosher salt

1 teaspoon dried rosemary

1 lemon, juiced

1/4 cup soy sauce

1/3 cup pineapple juice

2 tablespoons olive oil

Directions

Firstly, pat the salmon dry with paper towels. Season the salmon with black pepper, salt, and rosemary.

To make the marinade, in another bowl, combine together the lemon juice, soy sauce, pineapple juice, and olive oil.

Place the salmon in the marinade; transfer it to the refrigerator and let it sit at least 2 hours.

Lastly, lay the salmon fillets on an air fryer grill pan. Bake at 330 degrees F for 8 minutes. Enjoy!

99. Easy Herbed Steak

(Ready in about 50 minutes | Servings 4)

Ingredients

2 sprigs thyme, chopped

2 sprigs rosemary, chopped

4 cloves garlic, finely chopped

2 tablespoons extra-virgin olive oil

2 steaks

1/2 teaspoon salt

1/2 teaspoon smoked cayenne pepper

Freshly ground black pepper, to taste

Directions

In a bowl, thoroughly combine all ingredients, except the steaks. Let your steaks marinate for 30 minutes.

Roast at 400 degrees F for 15 to 20 minutes. Make sure to turn the steak halfway through the cooking time.

100. Garlic Sebago Potatoes with Bacon

(Ready in about 15 minutes | Servings 4)

Ingredients

4 Sebago potatoes, peeled and diced

4 slices bacon, diced

4 garlic cloves, peeled and smashed

1 teaspoon cayenne pepper

1/2 teaspoon sea salt

1/4 teaspoon ground black pepper

1 teaspoon cumin powder

1/2 teaspoon onion powder

1 tablespoon olive oil

Directions

Throw the potatoes into the pan. Now, cook them at 360 degrees F for 11 minutes.

Add the bacon and garlic; cook for 3 more minutes. Now, toss it with all seasonings. Drizzle olive oil over all. Serve and enjoy!

101. Grandma's Juicy Pork Chops

(Ready in about 1 hour 20 minutes | Servings 2)

Ingredients

2 large-sized pork chops

2 tablespoons extra-virgin olive oil

2 tablespoons lemon juice

2 teaspoons dried thyme

1 teaspoon onion powder

1 teaspoon white wine vinegar

1 tablespoon whole grain mustard

Salt and ground black pepper, to taste

Directions

Add all ingredients to a large resealable plastic bag. Allow the meat to marinate at least 1 hour.

After that, add the pork chops to the food basket. Cook for 20 minutes at 400 degrees F, turning once. Serve warm.

102. Tarragon Grilled Fish

(Ready in about 2 hours 10 minutes | Servings 2)

Ingredients

2 fish fillets

1/2 teaspoon kosher salt

1/4 teaspoon ground black pepper

1 teaspoon dried tarragon

1/4 teaspoon oregano

1/4 cup scallions, minced

1 lemon, juiced

1/4 cup soy sauce

1/3 cup dry white wine

1 tablespoon brown sugar

2 tablespoons olive oil

Directions

Season the fish fillets with the salt, black pepper, tarragon, and oregano.

To make the marinade, combine all remaining ingredients. Place the fish in the marinade; transfer it to the refrigerator; allow it to marinate at least 2 hours.

Lastly, arrange the fish fillets on an air fryer grill basket. Bake at 330 degrees F for 8 minutes. Serve warm.

103. Balsamic and Garlic Tenderloin Steak

(Ready in about 50 minutes | Servings 4)

Ingredients

1 tablespoon dried Italian seasoning, crushed

4 cloves garlic, finely chopped

1/2 cup beef broth

2 tablespoons extra-virgin olive oil

1 tablespoon balsamic vinegar

2 top sirloin steaks

1/2 teaspoon salt

1/2 teaspoon freshly ground black pepper

Directions

In a bowl, combine all ingredients, except the meat. Let the steaks marinate for 30 minutes.

Roast the steaks for about 20 minutes at 400 degrees F. Cooking time depends on how you like your steak.

Make sure to turn the steak halfway through the cooking time. Serve warm and enjoy!

104. Golden Roast Potatoes

(Ready in about 20 minutes | Servings 4)

Ingredients

1 pound potatoes, peeled and diced

Juice and zest of 1 lemon

3 garlic cloves, peeled and smashed

1/2 teaspoon sea salt

1/4 teaspoon ground black pepper

1 teaspoon fennel seeds

1 teaspoon celery seeds

1/2 teaspoon shallot powder

2 tablespoons butter

Directions

Toss the potatoes into the cooking basket. Roast them for 11 minutes at 360 degrees F.

Add lemon and garlic, and cook for an additional 3 more minutes.

Now, toss roasted potatoes with all seasonings. Dot with butter and serve warm.

105. Crispy Beef Schnitzel

(Ready in about 15 minutes | Servings 1)

Ingredients

1 beef schnitzel

Salt and ground black pepper, to taste

2 tablespoons olive oil

1/3 cup breadcrumbs

1 egg, whisked

Directions

Season the schnitzel with salt and black pepper.

In a mixing bowl, combine the oil and breadcrumbs. In another shallow bowl, beat the egg until frothy.

Dip the schnitzel in the egg; then, dip it in the oil mixture.

Air-fry at 350 degrees F for 12 minutes. Enjoy!

106. Roasted Chicken with Shallots

(Ready in about 20 minutes | Servings 4)

Ingredients

4 cloves garlic, minced

1 teaspoon smoked paprika

1/2 teaspoon freshly ground nutmeg

4 tablespoons olive oil

8 chicken breasts, boneless and skinless

1 shallot, sliced

Directions

In a bowl, mix all ingredients, except the shallots. Cover and refrigerate overnight.

Add the shallots to an air fryer basket. Lay the marinated chicken over it.

Bake at 370 degrees F for 20 minutes, turning halfway through. Serve with your favorite sauce.

107. Fried Tilapia with Zucchini

(Ready in about 15 minutes | Servings 4)

Ingredients

3/4 cup self- rising flour

1 tablespoon corn flour

3/4 teaspoon baking soda

1/2 teaspoon salt

1/4 teaspoon ground black pepper

20 ounces tilapia, cubed

2 zucchinis, thinly sliced

1/4 cup fresh cilantro leaves, chopped

Lemon wedges, to serve

Directions

Sift the flour and cornflour into a mixing bowl; add baking soda and salt; slowly whisk in chilled water to form a smooth batter.

Season tilapia and zucchini with the pepper; dip them in the batter.

Air-fry the fish and zucchini at 350 degrees F for about 15 minutes or until golden. Transfer them to a serving platter and top with fresh cilantro. Serve with lemon wedges.

108. Roasted Potatoes with Broccoli

(Ready in about 15 minutes | Servings 4)

Ingredients

4 potatoes, peeled and diced

1 small-sized head broccoli, cut into florets

2 garlic cloves, peeled and smashed

1 teaspoon smoked paprika

1/2 teaspoon sea salt

1/4 teaspoon ground black pepper

1/2 teaspoon shallot powder

2 tablespoons butter, melted

Directions

Throw the potatoes and broccoli florets into an air fryer basket. Now, cook them at 360 degrees F for 11 minutes.

Toss in the garlic and cook for 3 more minutes. Add all remaining ingredients and toss well to combine. Serve and enjoy!

109. Lime and Garlic Tilapia

(Ready in about 15 minutes | Servings 4)

Ingredients

2 cups Parmesan cheese, grated

2 garlic cloves, finely minced

Salt and ground black pepper, to taste

4 tilapia fillets

2 tablespoons lime juice

10 Ritz crackers, crushed

Directions

In a mixing bowl, combine Parmesan cheese, garlic, salt and black pepper until everything is well incorporated.

Then, drizzle tilapia fillets with the lime juice. Cover tilapia fillets with the cheese mixture; then, roll them over the breadcrumbs.

Bake at 330 F for about 12 minutes. Enjoy!

110. Easy Minute Steaks

(Ready in about 10 minutes | Servings 2)

Ingredients

2 minute steaks

1 teaspoon paprika

1/2 teaspoon sea salt

1/4 teaspoon ground black pepper, or to taste

2 tablespoons canola oil

10 Ritz crackers, crushed

2 eggs, whisked

Directions

Season the steaks with paprika, sea salt and ground black pepper.

In a mixing bowl, combine canola oil with crushed crackers. In a separate small-sized bowl, beat the eggs until frothy.

Dip the steaks in the egg; then, dip them in the oil/cracker mixture.

Air-fry for 10 minutes at 350 degrees F. Serve over mashed potatoes. Bon appétit!

111. Tender Beef with Sour Cream Sauce

(Ready in about 15 minutes | Servings 2)

Ingredients

9 ounces tender beef, chopped

1 cup scallions, chopped

2 cloves garlic, smashed

3/4 cup sour cream

3/4 teaspoon salt

1/4 teaspoon black pepper, or to taste

1/2 teaspoon dried dill weed

Directions

Add the beef, scallions, and garlic to the baking dish; cook for about 5 minutes at 390 degrees F.

Once the meat is starting to tender, pour in the sour cream. Stir in the salt, black pepper, and dill. Now, cook 7 minutes longer. Bon appétit!

112. Cajun Turkey Strips

(Ready in about 15 minutes | Servings 4)

Ingredients

1 cup corn meal mix

1 cup flour

2 tablespoons Cajun seasoning

1½ cups buttermilk

1 teaspoon soy sauce

1 turkey breasts, cut into strips

1/2 teaspoon salt

1/2 teaspoon ground black pepper, or to taste

Directions

Take three bowls. Combine the corn meal, 1/2 cup of the plain flour, and Cajun seasoning in the first bowl. Mix the buttermilk and soy sauce in the second bowl.

Season the turkey strips with the salt and black pepper. Now, dip each strip in the remaining 1/2 cup of flour, then in the buttermilk; lastly, cover them with the corn meal mixture.

Transfer the turkey to the air fryer baking pan and cook for 15 minutes at 350 degrees F. Enjoy!

113. Parmesan Balsamic Cod Fillets

(Ready in about 15 minutes | Servings 4)

Ingredients

2 cups Parmesan cheese, grated

2 garlic cloves, finely minced

1/2 teaspoon smoked paprika

Salt and ground black pepper, to taste

4 cod fillets

2 tablespoons balsamic vinegar

1 cup Italian seasoned breadcrumbs

Directions

In a mixing dish, combine Parmesan, garlic, paprika, salt and black pepper until everything is well incorporated.

Then, drizzle cod fillets with the balsamic vinegar. Cover tilapia fillets with the Parmesan mixture; then, roll them over breadcrumbs.

Bake at 330 degrees F for about 12 minutes. Bon appétit!

114. Onion and Thyme Steak

(Ready in about 15 minutes | Servings 4)

Ingredients

4 lean steaks, cut into strips

2 cloves garlic, minced

1 shallot, sliced

1 can tomatoes, crushed

3/4 cup French onion soup

2 sprigs fresh thyme, chopped

1/2 teaspoon sea salt

1/2 teaspoon ground black pepper, or to taste

Directions

Add the steaks, garlic, and shallots to the air fryer basket; then, cook for 10 minutes at 390 degrees F, working with batches and shaking occasionally.

Throw in the other ingredients and cook for an additional 5 minutes. Bon appétit!

115. Hoisin Herbed Chicken Breasts

(Ready in about 30 minutes | Servings 4)

Ingredients

1/4 cup sesame oil

4 cloves garlic, minced

2 tablespoons Hoisin sauce

1 tablespoon cooking wine

1 teaspoon fresh thyme leaves, minced

1/2 teaspoon fresh sage leaves, minced

1/2 teaspoon fresh rosemary leaves, minced

1/2 teaspoon seasoned salt

1/2 teaspoon freshly cracked black pepper

3 boneless chicken breasts, cut into small pieces

Directions

Warm the oil in a saucepan over medium-low heat. Then, sauté the garlic for just 1 minute, or until fragrant.

Remove the garlic from the heat; pour in the Hoisin sauce and wine. Now, add all seasonings. Pour the mixture into a baking dish.

Toss in the chicken breasts and roast for 30 minutes at 330 degrees F. Serve and enjoy!

116. Mint and Parmesan Steak

(Ready in about 15 minutes | Servings 4)

Ingredients

4 minute steaks

1 teaspoon smoked cayenne pepper

1/2 teaspoon sea salt

1/4 teaspoon ground black pepper, or to taste

2 tablespoons canola oil

1/4 cup finely grated parmesan

1/4 cup chopped fresh mint

1 ½ cups fresh breadcrumbs

2 eggs, whisked

Directions

Season your steaks with cayenne pepper, salt and black pepper.

In a mixing bowl, combine the oil, parmesan, mint, and breadcrumbs. In a separate small-sized bowl, beat the eggs until frothy.

Dip your steaks in the egg; then, dip it in the parmesan mixture.

Air-fry for 10 minutes at 350 degrees F, working in batches. Serve with your favorite salad. Bon appétit!

117. Family Beef Steaks with Beans

(Ready in about 15 minutes | Servings 4)

Ingredients

4 beef steaks, trim the fat and cut into strips

1 cup green onions, chopped

2 cloves garlic, minced

1 red bell pepper, seeded and thinly sliced

1 can tomatoes, crushed

1 can cannellini beans

3/4 cup beef broth

1/4 teaspoon dried basil

1/2 teaspoon cayenne pepper

1/2 teaspoon sea salt

1/4 teaspoon ground black pepper, or to taste

Directions

Add the steaks, green onions and garlic to the air fryer basket; then, cook at 390 degrees F for 10 minutes, working in batches.

Stir in the remaining ingredients and cook for an additional 5 minutes. Bon appétit!

118. Cheesy Stuffed Peppers

(Ready in about 20 minutes | Servings 4)

Ingredients

2 tablespoons olive oil

2 cloves garlic, minced

1 onion, finely chopped

1/2 cup ground pork

2 cups canned tomatoes, crushed

1 teaspoon dried oregano

1/2 teaspoon dried basil

1/2 cup rice, cooked

4 bell peppers, remove tops, membranes, and seeds

1/4 cup dry white wine, at room temperature

1/4 cup warm water

3/4 cup shredded mozzarella cheese

Directions

In a nonstick skillet, heat olive oil over medium heat. Then, sauté the garlic and onion until tender and fragrant; add ground pork and continue sautéing until the pork is browned; drain off excess fat.

Stir in 1 ½ cups tomatoes, oregano, basil, and cooked rice; give it a good stir.

Rinse the peppers. Divide the filling among bell peppers and add the tops. Arrange the peppers in a baking dish.

Whisk remaining 1/2 cup of tomatoes, wine, and water; pour this mixture into the baking dish. Cover and cook for 10 minutes at 370 degrees F. Uncover and cook for 10 more minutes. Serve topped with shredded mozzarella. Enjoy!

119. Garlicky Turkey with Dill Sauce

(Ready in about 1 hour 20 minutes | Servings 4)

Ingredients

10 cloves garlic, minced

1/2 teaspoon freshly ground nutmeg

4 tablespoons melted butter

1 medium-sized turkey breast, quartered

1 teaspoon shallot powder

Salt and ground black pepper, to your liking

1/2 teaspoon cayenne pepper

Fresh juice of 1 lemon

For the Sauce:

3/4 cup fresh dill, chopped

2 cups Greek yogurt

2 tablespoons mayonnaise

A pinch of cayenne pepper

Directions

In a mixing bowl, mix together the garlic, nutmeg, and melted butter; rub the turkey with the garlic mixture.

Add the shallot powder, salt, black pepper, cayenne pepper, and lemon juice. Cover and refrigerate at least 1 hour.

Preheat your air fryer to 370 degrees F. Roast the turkey in the air fryer basket for 20 minutes, turning halfway through; roast in batches as needed.

To make the dill sauce, mix all ingredients for the sauce. Serve the turkey with the dill sauce and enjoy!

120. Honey and Wine Chicken Breasts

(Ready in about 15 minutes | Servings 4)

Ingredients

2 chicken breasts, rinsed and halved

1 tablespoon melted butter

1/2 teaspoon freshly ground pepper, or to taste

3/4 teaspoon sea salt, or to taste

1 teaspoon paprika

1 teaspoon dried rosemary

2 tablespoons dry white wine

1 tablespoon honey

Directions

Firstly, pat the chicken breasts dry. Lightly coat them with the melted butter.

Then, add the remaining ingredients. Transfer them to the air fryer basket; bake about 15 minutes at 330 degrees F. Serve warm and enjoy!

121. Ricotta and Parsley Stuffed Turkey Breasts

(Ready in about 25 minutes | Servings 4)

Ingredients

1 turkey breast, quartered

1 cup Ricotta cheese

1/4 cup fresh Italian parsley, chopped

1 teaspoon garlic powder

1/2 teaspoon cumin powder

1 egg, beaten

1 teaspoon paprika

Salt and ground black pepper, to taste

Crushed tortilla chips

1 ½ tablespoons extra-virgin olive oil

Directions

Firstly, flatten out each piece of turkey breast with a rolling pin. Prepare three mixing bowls.

In a shallow bowl, combine Ricotta cheese with the parsley, garlic powder, and cumin powder.

Place the Ricotta/parsley mixture in the middle of each piece. Repeat with the remaining pieces of the turkey breast and roll them up.

In another shallow bowl, whisk the egg together with paprika. In the third shallow bowl, combine the salt, pepper, and crushed tortilla chips.

Dip each roll in the whisked egg, then, roll them over the tortilla chips mixture. Transfer prepared rolls to the air fryer basket. Drizzle olive oil over all.

Cook at 350 degrees F for 25 minutes, working in batches. Serve warm, garnished with some extra parsley, if desired.

122. Cheesy Chicken in Leek-Tomato Sauce

(Ready in about 20 minutes | Servings 4)

Ingredients

2 large-sized chicken breasts, cut in half lengthwise

Salt and ground black pepper, to taste

4 ounces Cheddar cheese, cut into sticks

1 tablespoon sesame oil

1 cup leeks, chopped

2 cloves garlic, minced

2/3 cup roasted vegetable stock

2/3 cup tomato puree

1 teaspoon dried rosemary

1 teaspoon dried thyme

Directions

Firstly, season chicken breasts with the salt and black pepper; place a piece of Cheddar cheese in the middle. Then, tie it using a kitchen string; drizzle with sesame oil and reserve.

Add the leeks and garlic to the oven safe bowl; cook in the air fryer at 390 degrees F for 5 minutes or until tender.

Add the reserved chicken. Throw in the other ingredients and cook for 12 to 13 minutes more or until the chicken is done. Enjoy!

123. Old-Fashioned Stuffed Peppers

(Ready in about 25 minutes | Servings 4)

Ingredients

1/2 cup rice

1 ¾ cups water

1/4 cup canola oil

1 onion, finely chopped

2 cloves garlic, minced

6 ounces ground beef

2 cups canned tomatoes, crushed

1 teaspoon dried oregano

1/2 teaspoon dried basil

1/2 teaspoon dried marjoram

4 red bell peppers

1/2 cup roasted vegetable stock

Directions

Microwave the rice with water for 4 minutes; reserve.

In a sauté pan, heat canola oil over medium flame. Then, sauté the onion, garlic and beef until the beef is browned; drain off excess fat.

Stir in 1½ cups of tomatoes, oregano, basil, marjoram and reserved rice; stir to combine well.

Slice off the tops of your peppers; now, remove the seeds. Divide the filling among the peppers and add the tops of peppers. Arrange the peppers in a baking dish.

Whisk remaining 1/2 cup of tomatoes with the stock; pour this mixture into the dish. Cover tightly with foil; cook for 10 minutes at 370 degrees F. Uncover and cook for 10 minutes longer. Serve and enjoy!

124. Turkey with Creamy Rosemary Sauce

(Ready in about 1 hour 20 minutes | Servings 4)

Ingredients

1 cup white wine

4 tablespoons melted butter, melted

1 pound turkey thighs, boneless, skinless, and cubed

2 cloves garlic, minced

1 teaspoon paprika

Salt and ground black pepper, to your liking

1 tablespoon balsamic vinegar

1 cup full fat sour cream

2 tablespoons mayonnaise

1 heaping tablespoon fresh rosemary, minced

Directions

In a large-sized mixing dish, combine together the wine, butter, and turkey. Now, stir in the garlic, paprika, salt, black pepper, and balsamic vinegar. Cover and refrigerate at least 1 hour.

Preheat your air fryer to 370 degrees F. Roast the turkey for 20 minutes, turning halfway through; work with batches.

To make the sauce, combine the sour cream with mayonnaise and rosemary. Serve the turkey with the rosemary sauce and enjoy!

125. Rosemary-Parmesan Fish Fillets

(Ready in about 15 minutes | Servings 4)

Ingredients

1/4 cup mayonnaise

1 ½ cups Parmesan cheese, grated

1/2 teaspoon red pepper flakes, crushed

2 rosemary sprigs, minced leaves

4 fish fillets

1/2 teaspoon sea salt

1 tablespoon orange juice

2 tablespoons balsamic vinegar

10 Ritz crackers, crushed

Directions

Mix the mayonnaise, Parmesan cheese, red pepper, and rosemary until blended.

Season the fish fillets with salt; drizzle them with the orange juice and balsamic vinegar.

Coat the fish fillets with the mayonnaise/cheese mixture; sprinkle them with cracker crumbs. Bake at 330 degrees F for about 12 minutes. Enjoy!

126. Roasted Chicken with Spinach Salad

(Ready in about 20 minutes | Servings 4)

Ingredients

4 chicken breasts, cut in half lengthwise

1/2 teaspoon paprika

Salt and ground black pepper, to taste

1 tablespoon olive oil

2 cloves garlic, minced

1 cup roasted vegetable stock

1 teaspoon dried thyme

For the Salad:

2 cups baby spinach

1/2 cup apple cider vinegar

1 tablespoon honey

1/4 cup extra-virgin olive oil

Kosher salt and ground black pepper, to taste

Directions

Season the chicken with the paprika, salt and black pepper; drizzle with the oil. Add the garlic, stock, and thyme, and gently stir to coat.

Now, roast your chicken at 390 degrees F for 15 to 18 minutes.

Meanwhile, prepare the salad by mixing all salad components. Serve the chicken with the prepared spinach salad. Enjoy!

127. Mustard Cider Pork Chops

(Ready in about 20 minutes | Servings 4)

Ingredients

4 center-cut loin pork chops

1 tablespoon whole grain mustard

1/2 cup apple cider vinegar

2 sprigs fresh thyme. chopped

1 tablespoon dried marjoram

Directions

Place the pork chops in the air fryer basket. Now, add the remaining ingredients and toss to coat well.

Roast at 400 degrees F for 20 minutes, turning once. Mound sautéed vegetables on a platter; top with prepared pork chops and serve.

128. Leftover Potato Casserole

(Ready in about 25 minutes | Servings 4)

Ingredients

4 large-sized potatoes, peeled and diced

4 slices leftover fully cooked ham, cubed

2 garlic cloves, peeled and smashed

1/2 teaspoon sea salt

1/4 teaspoon ground black pepper

1 teaspoon cumin powder

1/2 teaspoon shallot powder

1 tablespoon olive oil

1/4 cup breadcrumbs

Directions

Throw the potatoes into the air fryer cooking basket. Now, cook them at 360 degrees F for 11 minutes.

Add the ham and garlic, and toss them with all seasonings. Drizzle olive oil over all. Sprinkle breadcrumbs atop casserole. Cook for 10 more minutes.

Serve warm and enjoy!

129. Family Pork Chops and Potatoes

(Ready in about 30 minutes | Servings 4)

Ingredients

4 tablespoons canola oil

1 tablespoon fresh rosemary, chopped

1 tablespoon fresh coriander, chopped

1 teaspoon basil, dried

1 teaspoon sea salt

1/4 teaspoon freshly ground black pepper

1 teaspoon granulated garlic

2 teaspoons shallot powder

Grated rind of 1/2 orange

4 boneless pork chops

6 red potatoes, quartered

Directions

Prepare the rub for the meat, by mixing all ingredients, except the pork and potatoes. Set aside.

Then, evenly coat each pork chop with the prepared rub. Salt the potatoes to taste and arrange them in the bottom of the air fryer basket. Place the chops on top of the potatoes.

Roast for 30 minutes at 350 degrees F, turning halfway through. Enjoy!

130. Spicy Buttermilk-Fried Chicken Legs

(Ready in about 30 minutes | Servings 2)

Ingredients

2 chicken legs, rinsed

1 teaspoon sea salt

1 teaspoon black pepper

3/4 teaspoon dill weed, dried

1/4 teaspoon paprika

1 cup buttermilk

2 cups all-purpose flour

1 tablespoon baking powder

1 tablespoon onion powder

1/2 teaspoon sea salt

Directions

Toss together the chicken legs, salt, black pepper, dill, and paprika in a large-sized mixing bowl. Pour in the buttermilk; gently stir until it is well coated. Let it marinate for at least 6 hours in the fridge.

In a separate bowl, mix the remaining ingredients. Now, dredge the chicken in the seasoned flour.

Arrange the chicken in the fryer basket; spritz with an oil spray; transfer the basket to the air fryer. Bake at 370 degrees F for 20 minutes.

Then, turn the chicken pieces over, oil the other side and bake an additional 10 minutes. Serve warm.

131. Cajun Stuffed Portabella Mushrooms

(Ready in about 10 minutes | Servings 2)

Ingredients

4 portabella mushroom caps, scoop out insides

4 tablespoons melted butter

4 tablespoons tomato ketchup

4 tablespoons Colby cheese, grated

4 slices ham, chopped

1 tablespoon Cajun seasoning

Directions

Drizzle each mushroom cap with the melted butter. Divide the ketchup, cheese and ham among mushroom caps.

Transfer them to the cooking basket. Sprinkle Cajun seasonings over all stuffed mushrooms.

Cook for 5 minutes at 330 degrees F. Serve with a salad of choice. Enjoy!

132. Mushroom Pork Steaks

(Ready in about 50 minutes | Servings 2)

Ingredients

2 pork steaks

1 cup white mushrooms, sliced

2 tablespoons extra-virgin olive oil

3/4 teaspoon salt

1/2 teaspoon ground black pepper, to taste

1/2 teaspoon smoked cayenne pepper

1/2 (10.75-ounce) can condensed cream of mushroom soup

Directions

In a mixing dish, thoroughly combine all of the above ingredients. Let the mixture stand for about 30 minutes.

Roast the steak at 400 degrees F for 15 to 20 minutes. Make sure to turn the meat halfway through the cooking time. Serve warm.

133. Chicken and Cheese Tortillas

(Ready in about 25 minutes | Servings 4)

Ingredients

4 chicken legs

Kosher salt, to your liking

1/2 teaspoon shallot powder

1 teaspoon garlic powder

3/4 teaspoon chili powder

2 tablespoons olive oil

1/3 cup Colby cheese, shredded

1/4 cup roasted red peppers, julienned

1/4 cup lemon juice

1/4 cup scallions, chopped

12 corn tortillas

Directions

Season the chicken with salt, shallot powder, garlic powder and chili powder.

Drizzle olive oil over seasoned chicken legs. Then, cook your chicken in the air fryer for 25 minutes at 350 degrees F.

Next, shred the chicken and add the remaining ingredients. Assemble the tortillas and serve with guacamole.

134. Scalloped Potatoes au Gratin

(Ready in about 20 minutes | Servings 2)

Ingredients

2 large-sized russet potatoes, sliced

2 eggs, well-beaten

1/2 (10.75-ounce) can cream of mushroom soup

2 tablespoons buttermilk

1 tablespoon flour

1/2 teaspoon ground black pepper

1/4 teaspoon red pepper flakes, crushed

1/2 teaspoon sea salt

1/4 cup fresh cilantro, chopped

1/2 cup shredded Italian cheese blend

Directions

Arrange the potato slices in the bottom of the food basket; fry them for 10 minutes at 350 degrees F. Take the potatoes out of your air fryer.

In the meantime, prepare the topping by mixing the eggs, cream of mushroom soup, buttermilk, flour, black pepper, red pepper, and salt.

Cover the potatoes with the topping mixture; sprinkle fresh cilantro over it and top with the cheese blend; increase the temperature to 400 degrees F and cook for 10 minutes longer. Serve warm.

135. Roasted Pork Chops with Potatoes and Carrots

(Ready in about 30 minutes | Servings 4)

Ingredients

4 boneless pork chops

2 cloves garlic, peeled and halved

4 tablespoons extra-virgin olive oil

1 teaspoon basil, dried

1 teaspoon oregano, dried

1 teaspoon fresh or dried parsley

1/4 teaspoon freshly ground black pepper

1 teaspoon sea salt

1 teaspoon smoked cayenne pepper

1 teaspoon celery seeds

4 large-sized carrots, cut into sticks

6 red potatoes, quartered

Salt and red pepper flakes, to taste

Directions

Rub the chops with the garlic halves. In a mixing bowl, combine the oil, basil, oregano, parsley, black pepper, salt, cayenne pepper, and celery seeds.

Now, evenly coat each pork chop with the prepared herbed mixture. Season the carrots and potatoes with salt and red pepper flakes.

Place the carrots and potatoes on the bottom of the baking dish. Top with the pork chops.

Roast for 30 minutes at 350 degrees F, working in batches. Make sure to shake a few times and serve warm.

136. Aromatic Lavender Pork Steaks

(Ready in about 50 minutes | Servings 2)

Ingredients

2 pork steaks

1/4 cup olive oil

2 tablespoons fresh lavender, finely chopped

1 teaspoon fresh shopped rosemary

3/4 teaspoon salt

1/2 teaspoon ground black pepper, to taste

1/2 (10.75-ounce) can condensed cream of mushroom soup

Directions

Combine all of the above ingredients in the baking dish. Let the mixture stand at least 30 minutes.

Roast at 400 degrees F for 15 to 20 minutes or until the steaks are tender. Make sure to turn the steaks halfway through the cooking time. Serve warm.

137. Garlicky Roasted Veggies

(Ready in about 15 minutes | Servings 4)

Ingredients

4 potatoes, peeled and sliced

4 carrots, cut into coins

1 small-sized head broccoli, cut into florets

4 garlic cloves, peeled and smashed

1/2 teaspoon sea salt

1/4 teaspoon ground black pepper

1/2 teaspoon onion powder

2 tablespoons olive oil

Directions

Add the potato slices, carrot coins, and broccoli florets to an air fryer basket. Roast them approximately 12 minutes at 360 degrees F.

Toss in remaining items and cook for 3 minutes longer. Serve and enjoy!

138. Sage and Orange Pork Chops

(Ready in about 20 minutes | Servings 2)

Ingredients

2 center-cut loin pork chops

1 tablespoon fresh sage, finely minced

1/4 cup dry red wine

2 tablespoons orange juice

Paprika, to your liking

Salt and ground black pepper, to taste

Directions

Add all of the above items to a mixing dish. Toss to coat well.

Next, air-fry the pork for 20 minutes at 400 degrees F, turning once or twice. Garnish with fresh sage and serve.

139. Mustard Shrimp with Angel Hair Pasta

(Ready in about 10 minutes | Servings 4)

Ingredients

1 pound shrimp, shelled and deveined

2 tablespoons melted butter

1 tablespoon Dijon mustard

1/4 cup green onions, chopped

4 cloves garlic, finely minced

1/2 teaspoon sea salt

1/4 teaspoon freshly cracked black pepper

1/2 teaspoon dried thyme

Directions

In a mixing dish, combine all of the above items; stir until the shrimp is well coated.

Add your mixture to the cooking dish; air-fry approximately 5 minutes at 390 degrees F. Serve over angel hair pasta.

140. Creamy Ginger Chicken

(Ready in about 2 hours 15 minutes | Servings 4)

Ingredients

2 chicken breasts, cubed

1/2 cup Greek yogurt

2 tablespoons lemon juice

2 tablespoons olive oil

1 tablespoon ginger, grated

2 cloves garlic, minced

1/2 cup tomato puree

1/2 cup thickened cream

Salt and ground black pepper, to taste

Cayenne pepper, to taste

Directions

Mix all ingredients in a bowl; now, marinate the chicken for at least 2 hours.

Air-fry the chicken for 12 minutes at 350 degrees F. Serve with naan and enjoy!

141. Cilantro and Mint Steak

(Ready in about 2 hours 10 minutes | Servings 4)

Ingredients

1 pound steak, cut into four portions

1 cup fresh cilantro, finely chopped

1/4 cup mint, finely minced

4 garlic cloves, finely minced

1 teaspoon cayenne pepper

1 teaspoon ground cumin

1 cayenne pepper

1/2 teaspoon black pepper

1/2 cup olive oil

3 tablespoons vinegar

1 teaspoon salt

Directions

Pat steak dry with a kitchen towel. Combine all ingredients in a mixing bowl and refrigerate it for about 2 hours.

Cook for 10 minutes at 350 degrees F. Serve warm.

142. Chinese Pork Chops

(Ready in about 20 minutes | Servings 2)

Ingredients

2 center-cut loin pork chops

1 tablespoon Oyster sauce

1 tablespoon soy sauce

1 tablespoon brown sugar

2 tablespoons orange juice

1 tablespoon sesame oil

1 teaspoon Five-spice powder

Salt and ground black pepper, to taste

Directions

Add all of the above items to a mixing bowl. Toss until the pork chops are well coated.

Next, air-fry the pork for 20 minutes at 400 degrees F, turning once or twice. Enjoy!

143. Pork Ribs with Cherry Tomatoes

(Ready in about 1 hour 25 minutes | Servings 4)

Ingredients

1 rack of pork ribs

1 teaspoon baking soda

1 tablespoon dry white wine

1/2 teaspoon sea salt

1/2 teaspoon ground black pepper

1 tablespoon honey

1 tablespoon soy sauce

1 tablespoon cornstarch

1/2 teaspoon sesame oil

1 cloves garlic, minced

1/2 cup cherry tomatoes

Directions

Cut the ribs into single sections; transfer them to a serving bowl. Add the other ingredients, except for cherry tomatoes; toss to coat.

Let it marinate at least 1 hour. After that, toss in cherry tomatoes; air-fry the ribs for 20 to 25 minutes at 390 degrees F. Enjoy!

144. Roasted Drumsticks with Celery and Potatoes

(Ready in about 30 minutes | Servings 4)

Ingredients

4 tablespoons sesame oil

1 teaspoon cayenne pepper

1/4 teaspoon freshly ground black pepper

1 teaspoon sea salt

1 teaspoon celery seeds

1 teaspoon fennel seeds

1 teaspoon dried marjoram

4 chicken drumsticks

2 celery stalk, cut into coins

6 red potatoes, quartered

Salt and paprika, to your liking

1 cup green onions, halved

4 cloves garlic, peeled and halved

Directions

In a small-sized mixing dish, combine sesame oil, cayenne pepper, black pepper, salt, celery seeds, fennel seeds, and marjoram.

Now, evenly coat each drumstick with the prepared mixture. Season the celery and potatoes with salt and paprika.

Place the celery and potatoes on the bottom of the baking dish. Then, add green onions and garlic. Top with the seasoned drumsticks.

Roast the drumsticks and vegetables for 30 minutes at 350 degrees F, working with batches. Make sure to stir a few times. Bon appétit!

145. Pork Chops with Plums

(Ready in about 1 hour 20 minutes | Servings 2)

Ingredients

2 center-cut loin pork chops

1 tablespoon aged balsamic vinegar

1 tablespoon Worcestershire sauce

1 tablespoon soy sauce

1 tablespoon olive oil

4-5 ripe plums, chopped

1 tablespoon fresh rosemary, chopped

Salt and ground black pepper, to taste

Directions

Add all of the above items to a mixing bowl. Let marinate at least 1 hour.

Next, air-fry the pork for 20 minutes at 400 degrees F, turning once or twice. Enjoy!

146. Creamy Mustard Chicken

(Ready in about 15 minutes | Servings 4)

Ingredients

2 chicken breasts, cubed

Salt and ground black pepper, to taste

2 tablespoons creamy mustard

1/4 cup yogurt

1 tablespoon ginger, grated

2 cloves garlic, minced

1/2 cup tomato puree

1/2 cup reduced-fat thickened cooking cream

2 tablespoons olive oil

Steamed green beans, to serve

Directions

Season the chicken breasts with salt and ground black pepper. Then, place the chicken in a mixing bowl. Add the rest of the above ingredients, except for steamed green beans.

Then, marinate the chicken cubes for about 2 hours.

Air-fry the chicken for 12 minutes at 350 degrees F. Serve with steamed green beans.

FAST SNACKS

147. Crispy Green Tomatoes

(Ready in about 10 minutes | Servings 4)

Ingredients

2 eggs

1/2 cup milk

1 cup flour

1/2 cup cornmeal

1/2 cup crushed tortilla chips

1/2 teaspoon ground black pepper

1/4 teaspoon cayenne pepper

1 teaspoon salt

4 medium-sized green tomatoes, sliced

Directions

Prepare three bowls. In the first bowl, whisk the eggs together with milk until well combined. Add the flour to another bowl.

Combine the cornmeal, tortilla chips, black pepper, cayenne pepper, and salt in the third bowl. Coat the tomato slices with the flour; then, with the egg/milk mixture, and lastly, roll them in the cornmeal mixture.

Air fry at 340 degrees F for about 6 minutes. Enjoy!

148. Lemon-Tequila Shrimp Skewers

(Ready in about 40 minutes | Servings 4)

Ingredients

16 shrimps

2 cloves garlic, finely minced

1/4 teaspoon ground black pepper

1 teaspoon kosher salt

1/2 cup fresh lemon juice

1 tablespoon tequila

1 teaspoon cumin powder

1/2 teaspoon mustard seeds

2 tablespoons flour

2 eggs, beaten

1 cup Panko

Directions

In a mixing dish, combine all ingredients, except for Panko. Let it sit at least 30 minutes, stirring occasionally.

Then, coat marinated prawns with panko. Roll them to coat well.

Air-fry the shrimp for 8 minutes at 350 degrees F using the grill pan. Serve on skewers. Eat warm or at room temperature.

149. Garlic-Butter Stuffed Mushrooms

(Ready in about 15 minutes | Servings 4)

Ingredients

12 mushrooms

1/4 cup seasoned breadcrumbs

2 garlic cloves, minced

1 tablespoon butter, melted

1/2 teaspoon salt

1/4 teaspoon cayenne pepper

1/4 teaspoon ground black pepper

Directions

Begin by removing the stalks from your mushrooms. Then, combine other ingredients in a bowl.

Next step, fill the mushrooms with the breadcrumb mixture.

Air-fry at 390 degrees F for 10 minutes. Arrange stuffed mushrooms on a serving platter and serve with favorite sauce.

150. Cajun Potato Wedges

(Ready in about 25 minutes | Servings 4)

Ingredients

4 large-sized potatoes, cut into wedges

1 tablespoon butter, melted

1/4 teaspoon sea salt

1/4 teaspoon ground black pepper

1/2 teaspoon paprika

1 tablespoon Cajun spice

Directions

Put the potato wedges into your air fryer. Drizzle them with melted butter. Now, cook for 25 minutes at 375 degrees F.

Pause the air fryer and shake your potatoes a few times during the cooking process.

Add the seasonings and toss to coat. Serve and enjoy!

151. Cheesy Turkey Treats

(Ready in about 10 minutes | Servings 4)

Ingredients

2 tablespoons hot wing sauce

1/4 cup soft cheese

6 ounces cooked and diced turkey breasts

1 ½ ounces blue cheese, crumbled

Salt and ground black pepper, to taste

12 wonton wrappers

Directions

In a bowl, combine together the hot wing sauce and soft cheese. Throw in the turkey and blue cheese.

Season with salt and pepper to taste. Stir until everything is just combined.

Now, place 1 wonton wrapper in each mini muffin cup; you should create a cup. Fill each cup with the turkey mixture.

Bake at 330 degrees F for 10 minutes, or until they're golden brown. Enjoy!

152. Cheese Mushroom Appetizer

(Ready in about 15 minutes | Servings 4)

Ingredients

12 fresh mushrooms

1/2 cup cream cheese, softened

1/4 cup seasoned breadcrumbs

1 teaspoon Italian-style seasoning

2 garlic cloves, crushed

1 tablespoon olive oil

1/2 teaspoon salt

1/4 teaspoon ground black pepper

Directions

Firstly, remove the stalks from the mushrooms. Then, combine the remaining ingredients.

Fill the mushrooms with the cheese mixture.

Air-fry at 390 degrees F for 10 minutes. Serve and enjoy!

153. Sticky Garlic Wings

(Ready in about 20 minutes | Servings 6)

Ingredients

2 cloves garlic, finely minced

1 teaspoon ground cumin

1/2 teaspoon garlic salt

1/2 teaspoon freshly ground black pepper, or to taste

1 pound chicken wings

1 teaspoon white sugar

1 tablespoon soy sauce

Chili sauce, to serve

Directions

In a mixing dish, combine the garlic, cumin, garlic salt, and black pepper. Rub the chicken wings with the garlic mixture.

Place the chicken wings in the food basket; add the sugar and soy sauce. Air-fry the wings for 18 minutes at 350 degrees F or until they are thoroughly cooked. Serve with the chili sauce.

154. Shrimp Wrapped in Bacon

(Ready in about 35 minutes | Servings 6)

Ingredients

1 pound shrimp, peeled and deveined

Salt and ground black pepper, to taste

1 teaspoon paprika

1 pound bacon slices

Chili sauce, to your liking

Directions

Season the shrimp with salt, black pepper, and paprika.

Wrap one slice of bacon around the shrimp. Repeat with the remaining ingredients. Then, refrigerate for 30 minutes.

Air-fry at 350 degrees F for 5 to 7 minutes, working with batches. Transfer them to a paper towel to drain excess fat. Arrange the shrimp on a serving platter and serve with chili sauce on the side.

155. Homemade Banana Chips

(Ready in about 25 minutes | Servings 6)

Ingredients

Juice of 1 fresh lemon

1/3 cup water

4 bananas, peeled and sliced

1/4 teaspoon turmeric powder

1/4 teaspoon freshly grated nutmeg

Directions

Firstly, mix the lemon juice and water in a bowl. Soak the banana slices in this mixture for 10 minutes.

Add the banana slices to the cooking basket. Dust with turmeric powder and grated nutmeg. Air-fry at 350 degrees F for 15 minutes.

156. Cheese and Chili Appetizer Balls

(Ready in about 15 minutes | Servings 4)

Ingredients

1/2 pound soft cheese

1 green chili, finely chopped

2 tablespoons all-purpose flour

1 egg

Salt and ground black pepper, to taste

1/4 teaspoon chaat masala

1 tablespoon fresh chives, chopped

Breadcrumbs of 4 bread slices

2 tablespoons extra-virgin olive oil

Directions

Combine the cheese, green chili, flour, egg yolk, salt, black pepper, and chaat masala in a bowl. Stir in the chives and mix to combine.

Divide the mixture into 16 equal portions; now, using wet hands, shape each portion into a ball.

Then, beat the egg white in another mixing dish. In a separate mixing dish, combine the breadcrumbs and olive oil.

Carefully dip your balls in the egg white; roll them in the breadcrumb mixture. Then, air-fry the balls for 8 minutes at 390 degrees F; work with batches. Enjoy!

157. Vermouth Shrimp Skewers

(Ready in about 40 minutes | Servings 4)

Ingredients

16 shrimps

2 cloves garlic, finely minced

1 teaspoon kosher salt

1/2 teaspoon dry mango powder

1/4 cup fresh lime juice

2 tablespoons vermouth

2 tablespoons flour

2 eggs

2 tablespoons olive oil

1 cup breadcrumbs

Directions

Place the shrimp in a mixing dish; toss in the garlic, salt, and mango powder.

Now, add the lime juice, vermouth, and flour. Let it sit at least 30 minutes, turning occasionally.

Beat the egg in a shallow bowl. In another shallow bowl, combine the oil and breadcrumbs.

Then, dip marinated prawns in already beaten egg; then, coat them with the breadcrumb mixture. Air-fry the shrimp for 8 minutes at 350 degrees F. Serve the shrimp on skewers and enjoy!

158. Cinnamon Apple Chips
(Ready in about 25 minutes | Servings 8)

Ingredients

1/3 cup water

1/4 cup lime juice

A pinch of salt

1 tablespoon sugar

3 Golden Delicious apples, cored and thinly sliced

1/2 teaspoon ground cinnamon

Directions

Combine the water, lime juice, salt and sugar in the mixing bowl. Soak the apple slices in this mixture for 5 to 10 minutes.

Air-fry the apple slices at 350 degrees F for 15 minutes. Dust with ground cinnamon and serve.

159. Turkey Zucchini Cocktail Meatballs
(Ready in about 50 minutes | Servings 10)

Ingredients

1 pound ground turkey

1 large-sized zucchini, grated

1 cup scallions, finely chopped

2 cloves garlic, minced

1/2 teaspoon dried oregano

1/2 teaspoon dried basil

1 teaspoon dried marjoram

1 egg

3/4 cup seasoned breadcrumbs

1/2 teaspoon red pepper flakes, crushed

1/2 teaspoon salt

1/2 teaspoon black pepper, or to taste

1 cup plain flour

Directions

Place ground turkey, along with the zucchini, scallions and garlic in a large-sized mixing bowl.

Then, stir in the oregano, basil, marjoram, egg, breadcrumbs, red pepper, salt, and black pepper.

Shape the mixture into even balls; refrigerate for about 30 minutes. Roll the balls in the flour.

Then, air-fry the balls at 350 degrees F for about 20 minutes, shaking once or twice; work with batches. Arrange on a serving platter and serve with currant jelly sauce, if desired.

160. Ham and Cheese Muffins

(Ready in about 20 minutes | Servings 6)

Ingredients

1 tablespoon melted butter

6 slices ham

1 box muffin mix

1 tablespoon Mediterranean dried herbs mix

2 cloves garlic, minced

1/3 cup Cheddar cheese, shredded

Directions

Firstly, melt the butter in a cast-iron skillet over medium-high flame. Then, cook the ham for about 5 minutes, until cooked through. Chop the ham and reserve.

Prepare the muffin mix according to the manufacturer's instructions. Stir in dried herbs mix and garlic; throw in Cheddar cheese and reserved ham.

Transfer the mixture to the mini muffin pan; bake at 330 degrees F for about 15 minutes. Serve at room temperature.

161. Crispy Sweet Onion Straws

(Ready in about 30 minutes | Servings 8)

Ingredients

2 sweet onions, thinly sliced

1 large-sized dish of ice water

1 cup all-purpose flour

1/2 teaspoon red pepper flakes, crushed

1/2 teaspoon garlic salt

1/2 teaspoon white pepper

1 teaspoon cumin powder

Nonstick cooking spray

Directions

Firstly, allow the onions to soak in the water for at least 15 minutes.

Place the flour, red pepper, salt, white pepper, and cumin powder in a zip lock bag. Drain the onion slices and transfer them to the bag; shake it well.

Lay the onions on the bottom of the cooking basket. Brush them with a nonstick cooking spray.

Bake at 410 degrees F for 14 minutes; turn them halfway through the cooking time and brush with cooking spray. Arrange on a serving platter and serve.

162. Turkey and Rice Balls

(Ready in about 2 hours 10 minutes | Servings 8)

Ingredients

1 pound ground turkey

1 onion, finely chopped

2 garlic cloves, finely minced

3 cups rice, cooked

4 eggs

1/3 melted butter

1 cup Feta cheese, crumbled

1 cumin powder

Salt and ground black pepper, to taste

1 cup seasoned breadcrumbs

Directions

Firstly, preheat a nonstick skillet over medium heat. Then, cook the ground turkey with onion and garlic until they're browned.

Stir in the rice, 3 eggs, butter, cheese, cumin powder, salt, and ground black pepper. Refrigerate at least 2 hours.

Shape the mixture into bite-sized balls. Beat the remaining 1 egg in a bowl; add seasoned breadcrumbs to another bowl.

Dip each ball in the egg; then, roll them over the breadcrumbs. Air-fry at 390 degrees F for about 5 minutes, working with batches. Serve and enjoy!

163. Chinese-Style Kale Chips

(Ready in about 5 minutes | Servings 8)

Ingredients

2 heads of kale

2 tablespoons sesame oil

1 tablespoon soy sauce

1 teaspoon Five-spice powder

Directions

Tear the kale leaves up into bite-sized pieces. Drizzle sesame oil and soy sauce over kale leaves. Season with Five-spice powder. Air-fry at 200 degrees F for about 3 minutes.

164. Hot and Spicy Crab Sticks

(Ready in about 12 minutes | Servings 4)

Ingredients

1 packet crab sticks, cut into small chunks

1 tablespoon olive oil

1 teaspoon chili powder

Directions

Place crab sticks in a bowl and toss them with olive oil. Add chili powder and toss again to combine well.

Air-fry crab sticks at 160 degrees F for 12 minutes or until golden brown; make sure to toss a few times. Serve with your favorite dipping sauce.

165. Aromatic Tamari Chicken Wings

(Ready in about 40 minutes | Servings 4)

Ingredients

1 teaspoon fresh rosemary

1 teaspoon fresh thyme

1 teaspoon fresh basil

1 teaspoon fresh sage

2 cloves garlic, finely minced

1 pound chicken wings

1 tablespoon tamari sauce

Directions

Place the herbs in the air fryer basket. Bake at 170 degrees F for 20 minutes.

Then, rub the chicken wings with the garlic and herb mixture. Drizzle tamari sauce over the wings.

Air-fry the wings for 18 minutes at 350 degrees F or until they are thoroughly cooked.

166. Spiced Appetizer Meatballs

(Ready in about 2 hours 10 minutes | Servings 8)

Ingredients

1 pound ground pork

2 garlic cloves, finely minced

1 cup green onions, finely chopped

3 cups rice, cooked

4 eggs

1/3 melted butter

1 cup Parmesan cheese, crumbled

1 mustard seeds

1 teaspoon cayenne pepper

1/2 teaspoon sea salt

1/4 teaspoon ground black pepper, to taste

1 teaspoon parsley flakes

1 teaspoon Italian seasoning

1 cup seasoned breadcrumbs

Directions

Cook the pork with garlic and green onions in a sauté pan.

Add the rice, 3 eggs, butter, Parmesan cheese, mustard seeds, cayenne pepper, salt, and ground black pepper. Refrigerate approximately 2 hours.

Shape the mixture into bite-sized balls with wet hands. Whisk the remaining 1 egg in a shallow bowl; in another bowl, combine the parsley flakes, Italian seasoning, and breadcrumbs.

Dip each ball in the whisked egg; then, roll them over the breadcrumb mixture. Air-fry at 390 degrees F for about 5 minutes, working with batches. Serve with toothpicks.

167. Frizzled Celery with Chili-Mayo Sauce

(Ready in about 45 minutes | Servings 8)

Ingredients

2 large-sized celery stalks, spiralized

Large dish with ice water

1 cup rice flour

Kosher salt and ground black pepper, to your liking

1 teaspoon cayenne pepper

1 teaspoon garlic powder

1 teaspoon onion powder

Melted coconut oil, for brushing

For the Sauce:

1 cup mayonnaise

3 tablespoons chili sauce

1/4 teaspoon smoked paprika

Directions

Allow the celery to soak in ice water for at least 30 minutes.

Add the rice flour, salt, black pepper, cayenne pepper, garlic powder, and onion powder to a resealable bag. Drain the celery and place them in the dry flour mixture. Toss to coat well.

Arrange the celery on the bottom of the air-fryer basket. Grease them with melted coconut oil.

Bake at 410 degrees F for 14 minutes; turn them halfway through the cooking time and grease them with coconut oil again.

In the meantime, combine all ingredients for the sauce. Chill the sauce and serve with frizzled celery.

168. Broccoli Snack Bites

(Ready in about 20 minutes | Servings 8)

Ingredients

2 pounds broccoli florets

2 tablespoons extra-virgin olive oil

1 teaspoon garlic salt

3/4 teaspoon ground black pepper

1/2 teaspoon dried dill weed

1/2 teaspoon cayenne pepper

1 tablespoon fresh chives

Directions

Bring a pan with 6 cups of water to a boil. Once boiling, add the broccoli and boil for about 4 minutes. Then, drain the broccoli florets; toss them with the olive oil and all seasonings.

Then, cook the broccoli at 400 degrees F for 15 minutes; make sure to shake it halfway through the cooking process.

Toss with chopped chives and serve right away.

169. Corn Muffin with Chorizo

(Ready in about 20 minutes | Servings 8)

Ingredients

1 tablespoon olive oil

3 Chorizo sausage, chopped

1 box corn muffin mix

1 teaspoon dried basil

1 teaspoon dried rosemary

1 teaspoon dried sage

1/4 cup shallots, chopped

1/3 cup Mozzarella cheese, shredded

Directions

Heat the olive oil in a skillet over medium-high heat. Then, cook Chorizo for about 5 minutes until cooked through. Chop the sausage and set it aside.

Prepare the muffin mix according to the package directions. Stir in the other ingredients, along with reserved sausage.

Transfer the mixture to the mini muffin pan; bake at 330 degrees F for about 15 minutes. Bon appétit!

170. Bacon-Wrapped Dates

(Ready in about 10 minutes | Servings 8)

Ingredients

1/2 pound dates, pitted

1/2 pound thin bacon slices

4 ounces Cheddar cheese

Directions

Wrap each date with a piece of bacon and piece of Cheddar cheese; secure them with a toothpick.

Bake for about 10 minutes at 330 degrees F.

171. Rosemary Potatoes with Dill Sauce

(Ready in about 10 minutes | Servings 4)

Ingredients

4 medium-sized potatoes, cut into thin slices

Nonstick cooking spray

1/2 teaspoon sea salt

1/2 teaspoon ground black pepper

1 teaspoon fresh rosemary, chopped

For the Dill Dip:

1/2 cup sour cream

1/2 cup mayonnaise

1/4 cup shallot, finely chopped

1 teaspoon dried dill

Directions

Brush the potatoes with a nonstick cooking spray. Season with salt, black pepper, and chopped rosemary.

Arrange the potato slices in an air fryer basket. Bake at 400 degrees F for 5 minutes. Pause and shake the potatoes. Bake an additional 5 minutes or until crisp.

Meanwhile, prepare the sauce by mixing all sauce items. Serve your potatoes with chilled sauce.

172. Basil and Rosemary Squash Bites

(Ready in about 20 minutes | Servings 8)

Ingredients

2 pounds squash, peeled, seeded, and cubed

1/4 cup brown sugar

2 tablespoons butter, melted

1 teaspoon basil, minced

1 teaspoon rosemary, minced

Directions

In a mixing bowl, place all of the above ingredients. Toss until everything is well coated.

Roast at 330 degrees F for 10 minutes. Pause the machine and toss the squash.

Now, increase the temperature to 400 degrees F and bake for another 10 minutes. Serve at room temperature.

173. Carrot and Beef Cocktail Balls

(Ready in about 50 minutes | Servings 10)

Ingredients

1 pound ground beef

2 carrots

1 red onion, peeled and chopped

2 cloves garlic

1/2 teaspoon dried rosemary, crushed

1/2 teaspoon dried basil

1 teaspoon dried oregano

1 egg

3/4 cup breadcrumbs

1/2 teaspoon salt

1/2 teaspoon black pepper, or to taste

1 cup plain flour

Directions

Place ground beef in a large bowl. In a food processor, pulse the carrot, onion and garlic; transfer the vegetable mixture to a large-sized bowl.

Then, add the rosemary, basil, oregano, egg, breadcrumbs, salt, and black pepper.

Shape the mixture into even balls; refrigerate for about 30 minutes. Roll the balls into the flour.

Then, air-fry the balls at 350 degrees F for about 20 minutes, turning occasionally; work with batches. Serve with toothpicks.

174. Restaurant-Style Frizzled Onions

(Ready in about 1 hour 15 minutes | Servings 8)

Ingredients

2 large-sized onions, thinly sliced

3 cups buttermilk

2 cups all-purpose flour

1/2 teaspoon chili powder

1/2 teaspoon kosher salt

1/2 teaspoon black pepper, preferably freshly cracked

Directions

Place the onions and buttermilk in a large bowl and let it stand at least 1 hour.

Combine the other ingredients in another mixing bowl. Drain the onions and place them in the dry mixture. Toss to coat well.

Arrange the onions on the bottom of the cooking basket. Treat them with a nonstick cooking spray.

Bake at 410 degrees F for 14 minutes; turn them halfway through the cooking time and treat with cooking spray again. Serve with your favorite sauce for dipping.

175. Japanese Furikake Sweet Potato Appetizer

(Ready in about 15 minutes | Servings 4)

Ingredients

4 sweet potatoes, peeled

1/4 cup bourbon

1 egg, beaten

1/4 cup sugar

1 tablespoon ghee

1 teaspoon furikake

Directions

Boil sweet potatoes until fork tender.

Thoroughly combine all ingredients with an electric mixer.

Scrape the mixture into a baking dish. Bake at 330 degrees F for 15 minutes. Enjoy!

176. Meatballs with Mango Glaze

(Ready in about 2 hours 10 minutes | Servings 8)

Ingredients

For the Meatballs:

1 pound mixed ground meat

2 garlic cloves, finely minced

1 cup leeks, finely chopped

2 eggs

1 teaspoon hot sauce

2 tablespoons lard, at room temperature

1 cup Parmesan cheese, crumbled

1/2 teaspoon sea salt

1/4 teaspoon ground black pepper, to taste

1 teaspoon smoked paprika

1 cup seasoned breadcrumbs

For the Mango Glaze:

1 mango, peeled and cubed

1/2 cup water

1/2 cup balsamic vinegar

1/4 cup honey

2 tablespoons unsalted butter

Directions

Brown ground meat along with the garlic and leeks.

Add the eggs, hot sauce, lard, Parmesan cheese, salt, ground black pepper and smoked paprika. Refrigerate approximately 2 hours.

Shape the mixture into bite-sized balls using wet hands. Add breadcrumbs to a shallow bowl.

Roll each ball over the breadcrumb and cook approximately 5 minutes at 390 degrees F.

In the meantime, in your food processor, pulse all ingredients for the mango glaze, except for butter.

Then, sauté this mixture in a saucepan; bring to a simmer and cook about 5 minutes or until the sauce has thickened. Fold in the butter and gently stir to combine.

Serve the meatballs with the mango glaze for dipping and enjoy!

176. Japanese Furikake Sweet Potato Appetizer

(Ready in about 15 minutes | Servings 4)

Ingredients

4 sweet potatoes, peeled

1/4 cup bourbon

1 egg, beaten

1/4 cup sugar

1 tablespoon ghee

1 teaspoon furikake

Directions

Boil sweet potatoes until fork tender.

Thoroughly combine all ingredients with an electric mixer.

Scrape the mixture into a baking dish. Bake at 330 degrees F for 15 minutes. Enjoy!

177. Zucchini and Carrot Bites

(Ready in about 20 minutes | Servings 6)

Ingredients

1 zucchini, grated

1 tablespoon sea salt

1 large-sized carrot, shredded

1/2 cup scallions, minced

1 tablespoon fresh parsley, chopped

1 tablespoon fresh sage, chopped

1 egg, lightly beaten

3/4 cup grated Romano cheese

1/4 cup rice flour

Directions

Grate the zucchini into a colander and toss with salt; let it stand for 10 minutes.

Drain and rinse the zucchini; use a paper towel to remove the excess water. Then, mix the zucchini with the remaining ingredients.

Take 1 tablespoon of the mixture at a time; shape it into a ball. Flatten each ball and brush it with a nonstick cooking spray.

Bake your cakes in a single layer at 330 degrees F for 10 minutes or until golden.

178. Parmesan Cauliflower Snack

(Ready in about 20 minutes | Servings 8)

Ingredients

1 large-sized head of cauliflower, broken into florets

2 tablespoons canola oil

2 sprigs thyme

3/4 teaspoon ground black pepper

1 teaspoon seasoned salt

1/2 teaspoon cayenne pepper

1/2 cup Parmesan cheese, grated

Directions

Firstly, boil cauliflower florets for about 4 minutes. Then, drain the cauliflower florets and toss them with the oil and all seasonings.

Place the cauliflower florets in the baking dish; scatter grated Parmesan cheese over it.

Roast at 400 degrees F for 15 minutes; turn it halfway through the cooking process. Serve immediately.

179. Cheese and Bacon Muffin Cups

(Ready in about 10 minutes | Servings 8)

Ingredients

2 cups Romano cheese, grated

1/2 cup mayonnaise

1 teaspoon cumin powder

1 teaspoon chili powder

4 slices bacon, cooked and crumbled

1 can large flaky-style biscuit dough

Directions

In a large-sized mixing bowl, combine Romano cheese and mayonnaise. Then, mix in the cumin powder, chili powder, and bacon.

Cut out biscuit dough with a knife to form biscuit pockets. Press the biscuit pockets into the bottom and up the sides of the muffin cups. Divide the mixture among cups.

Bake at 300 degrees F for about 10 minutes or until golden brown. Allow them to stand for a few minutes before removing from the cups. Enjoy!

180. Hot and Spicy Frizzled Carrots

(Ready in about 1 hour 15 minutes | Servings 6)

Ingredients

2 large-sized horse carrots, spiralized

3 cups buttermilk

2 cups all-purpose flour

Kosher salt and ground black pepper, to your liking

1/2 teaspoon chili powder

1 garlic clove, minced

Melted coconut oil, for brushing

Directions

Add the carrots to the buttermilk; allow them to soak at least 1 hour.

In a separate bowl, combine the flour, salt, black pepper, chili powder, and minced garlic. Drain the carrots and place them in the flour mixture. Toss to coat well.

Arrange the carrots on the bottom of the cooking basket. Brush them with some coconut oil.

Bake at 410 degrees F for 14 minutes; turn them halfway through the cooking time and grease them with coconut oil again. Plate up and enjoy!

181. Baby Spinach Chips

(Ready in about 5 minutes | Servings 8)

Ingredients

1 tablespoon olive oil

3 cups baby spinach leaves

Salt and ground black pepper, to taste

1 teaspoon garlic powder

Directions

Drizzle olive oil over spinach leaves.

Season with salt, black pepper, and garlic powder. Air-fry at 200 degrees F for 3 to 4 minutes.

182. Baked Camembert with Dates and Walnuts

(Ready in about 15 minutes | Servings 6)

Ingredients

4 tablespoons plum jam

1/3 cup dried dates, pitted and chopped

1 cup walnuts, chopped

13 ounces Camembert cheese

Directions

Place the jam in a microwave-safe dish. Microwave for 30 seconds.

In a mixing bowl, combine the dried dates with the walnuts. Add 1/2 of the jam and mix well to combine.

Place the round of Camembert in an oven-safe dish. Coat the cheese with the remaining 1/2 of the jam. Top the cheese with the date mixture.

Place the dish in the air fryer basket. Bake for 10 minutes at 325 degrees F. Serve with dippers of choice and enjoy!

183. Creamed Kale and Artichoke Dip

(Ready in about 15 minutes | Servings 10)

Ingredients

1 (8-ounce) package cream cheese

1/4 cup mayonnaise

1/4 cup grated Parmesan cheese

2 cloves garlic, minced

1/2 teaspoon cumin powder

1/2 teaspoon dried basil

1/2 teaspoon sea salt

1/2 teaspoon ground black pepper

1/2 teaspoon cayenne pepper

1/2 (14-ounce) can artichoke hearts, drained and chopped

2 cups kale leaves, torn into pieces

1/3 cup Mozzarella cheese, shredded

Directions

Combine together the cream cheese, mayonnaise, Parmesan, garlic, cumin powder, basil, salt, ground black pepper, and cayenne pepper.

Gently stir in the artichoke hearts and kale. Transfer the mixture to a baking dish. Scatter the Mozzarella cheese over the top.

Bake for 15 minutes at 330 degrees F. Serve with pita chips.

184. Mozzarella Bacon Muffins

(Ready in about 15 minutes | Servings 10)

Ingredients

1 tablespoon canola oil

6 slices bacon

1 box corn muffin mix

1 teaspoon cayenne pepper

1/2 teaspoon cumin powder

1/2 teaspoon chili powder

2 tablespoons green onions, chopped

1/3 cup Mozzarella cheese, shredded

Directions

Heat the oil in a cast-iron skillet over medium-high flame. Then, brown the bacon for about 5 minutes until crisp.

Remove from the heat and drain the bacon on a paper towel. Chop the bacon and reserve.

Prepare the muffin mix according to the manufacturer's instructions. Stir in the remaining ingredients; stir in the reserved bacon.

Scrape the mixture into the mini muffin pan; bake at 330 degrees F for about 15 minutes.

185. Swiss Chard Chips

(Ready in about 5 minutes | Servings 8)

Ingredients

1 tablespoon extra-virgin olive oil

2 cups Swiss chard leaves, torn into pieces

1 teaspoon kosher salt

1/2 teaspoon ground black pepper, or to taste

1 teaspoon shallot powder

1/2 teaspoon cumin powder

1 teaspoon garlic powder

Directions

Drizzle olive oil over chard leaves; toss to coat well.

Add all seasonings and toss again. Air-fry for 3 to 4 minutes at 200 degrees F. Serve with your favorite dipping sauce. Enjoy!

186. Roasted Acorn Squash with Tahini Sauce

(Ready in about 20 minutes | Servings 8)

Ingredients

2 large acorn squashes, peeled, seeded, and cubed

4 tablespoons brown sugar

2 tablespoons butter, melted

1 teaspoon grated nutmeg

2 tablespoons fresh lime juice

1 tablespoon tahini

Directions

In a mixing bowl, toss together the squash, sugar, butter, and nutmeg.

Air-fry at 330 degrees F for 10 minutes. Pause the machine and toss the squash again. Turn the temperature to 400 degrees F and bake for another 10 minutes.

In the meantime, prepare the sauce by mixing lime juice and tahini. Serve roasted squash with the sauce.

187. Potato Skins with Gruyère and Bacon

(Ready in about 15 minutes | Servings 4)

Ingredients

4 russet potatoes

1/2 cup Gruyère cheese, shredded

3 strips bacon, cooked and crumbled

2 tablespoons mayonnaise

1/2 cup sour cream

1/2 cup fresh chives, finely chopped

Directions

Microwave the potatoes until they are thoroughly cooked.

Cut them in half horizontally. Now, carefully scoop out the insides with a spoon, leaving about 1/4-inch potato on the skin.

Arrange the potato shells inside the cooking basket; lightly grease them with cooking spray. Bake at 400 degrees F for 10 minutes.

Add the cheese and crumbled bacon. Bake for another 2 minutes. In a small mixing bowl, combine the mayo and sour cream. Top with a dollop of mayo mixture and sprinkle with fresh chives.

188. Homemade Potato Chips

(Ready in about 40 minutes | Servings 4)

Ingredients

4 medium-sized potatoes, thinly sliced

Nonstick cooking spray

Salt and crushed red pepper, to your liking

Directions

Soak the potato slices in the cold water for 30 minutes.

Place the potatoes on a kitchen towel and dry them. Rub them with a cooking spray on all sides. Season with salt and red pepper.

Bake in an air fryer basket at 400 degrees F for 5 minutes. Pause the machine and toss. Bake for another 5 minutes or until they're crisp.

189. Buttery Mushroom Snack

(Ready in about 20 minutes | Servings 6)

Ingredients

1 pound mushrooms

2 tablespoons melted butter

1 teaspoon celery seeds

1 teaspoon garlic salt

1 tablespoon Mediterranean herb blend

2 tablespoons dry white wine

Directions

In a mixing dish, toss the mushrooms with the remaining ingredients.

Air-fry them for 8 minutes at 350 degrees F.

Pause the machine, stir the mushrooms and cook for another 8 minutes. Serve and enjoy!

190. Ricotta and Pepperoni Dipping Sauce

(Ready in about 15 minutes | Servings 12)

Ingredients

1 cup Ricotta cheese, room temperature

2 tablespoons mayonnaise

1 teaspoon Dijon mustard

1/4 cup sour cream

1 teaspoon oregano

1/2 teaspoon red pepper flakes

2 garlic cloves, finely minced

1/2 cup tomato puree

1 cup pepperoni, chopped

3/4 cup mozzarella cheese, shredded

Directions

In a large-sized bowl, whisk together all the ingredients, except for mozzarella.

Then, scrape the mixture into a shallow ovenproof dish.

Bake at 330 degrees F for 10 minutes or until bubbly. Scatter shredded mozzarella over the top. Bake for 5 minutes longer. Serve hot with dippers of choice.

191. Coriander Crispy Wings

(Ready in about 25 minutes | Servings 4)

Ingredients

1 tablespoon coriander, ground

1 teaspoon smoked paprika

1 teaspoon fresh sage

1 teaspoon garlic powder

2 teaspoons all-purpose flour

1 pound chicken wings

Directions

Toss all ingredients in a baking dish.

Air-fry the wings for 25 minutes at 350 degrees F. Bon appétit!

192. Spicy Potato Skins

(Ready in about 20 minutes | Servings 6)

Ingredients

4 Idaho baking potatoes

8 ounces thick-cut bacon, diced

1/2 cup Cottage cheese, softened

1 tablespoon salsa

1 tablespoon grated parmesan cheese

Directions

Microwave potatoes until they are thoroughly cooked. Then, scoop out the insides, leaving about 1/4-inch potato on the skin.

Arrange the potato skins on the bottom of the cooking basket; lightly grease them with a cooking spray. Bake at 400 degrees F for 10 minutes.

Add the bacon and Cottage cheese. Bake an additional 2 minutes. Sprinkle with salsa and parmesan and serve.

193. Potato Chips with Shallot Dip

(Ready in about 40 minutes | Servings 4)

Ingredients

4 medium-sized potatoes, thinly sliced

Nonstick cooking spray

Sea salt, to taste

1 shallot, thinly sliced

1/4 cup mayonnaise

1/4 cup soft cheese

1 cup sour cream

Directions

Soak the potato slices in the cold water for 30 minutes.

Place the potatoes on a kitchen towel and dry them. Rub them with a cooking spray on all sides. Season with salt.

Bake in an air fryer basket at 400 degrees F for 5 minutes. Pause the machine and toss. Bake for another 5 minutes or until they're crisp. Work with batches.

Meanwhile, make the dipping sauce by mixing the remaining ingredients. Serve your chips with the prepared dip. Enjoy!

194. Mouth-Watering Balsamic Mushrooms

(Ready in about 20 minutes | Servings 4)

Ingredients

1 pound mushrooms

3 tablespoons balsamic vinegar

3 tablespoons white wine

2 tablespoons olive oil

1/2 teaspoon black pepper, preferably freshly cracked

1 teaspoon salt

1 tablespoon dried thyme

Directions

In a mixing dish, toss all ingredients.

Air-fry them at 350 degrees F for 8 minutes.

Pause the machine, stir the mushrooms and cook for 8 more minutes. Bon appétit!

195. Pepperoni Stuffed Mushrooms

(Ready in about 10 minutes | Servings 6)

Ingredients

20 large-sized mushrooms, stalks removed

2 tablespoons butter, melted

1 yellow onion, finely chopped

3/4 cup pepperoni, diced

1/4 cup grated Parmesan cheese

2 garlic cloves, minced

1/2 teaspoon salt

1/4 teaspoon cayenne pepper

Directions

Place all mushrooms on a clean surface. Thoroughly combine other ingredients in a bowl.

Now, fill the mushrooms with the stuffing mix. Air-fry at 390 degrees F for 10 minutes. Bon appétit!

196. Ham and Feta Bites

(Ready in about 10 minutes | Servings 6)

Ingredients

1/4 cup Cottage cheese

2 tablespoons soy sauce

6 ounces ham, cooked and diced

1 ½ ounces Feta cheese, crumbled

1 teaspoon cayenne pepper

Salt and ground black pepper, to taste

12 wonton wrappers

Directions

In a mixing bowl, combine Cottage cheese and soy sauce. Now, add the ham and Feta cheese.

Season with cayenne pepper, salt, and ground black pepper to taste. Stir until it is just combined.

Now, place 1 wonton wrapper in each mini muffin cup. Fill each cup with the prepared mixture.

Bake at 330 degrees F for 10 minutes. Bon appétit!

197. Cilantro-Garlic Potato Snack

(Ready in about 25 minutes | Servings 4)

Ingredients

4 medium-sized russet potatoes, cut into wedges

1 tablespoon extra-virgin olive

1/2 lemon, juiced

2 cloves garlic, finely minced

1/4 teaspoon sea salt

1/4 teaspoon ground black pepper

1/4 cup fresh chopped cilantro

Directions

Rub the potato wedges with extra-virgin olive oil.

Now, add the lemon juice and garlic. Roast the potatoes for 25 minutes at 375 degrees F. Turn your potatoes a few times during the cooking process.

Season with salt and black pepper and top with fresh cilantro. Bon appétit!

198. Vidalia Sweet Potato Snack

(Ready in about 25 minutes | Servings 4)

Ingredients

4 cups sweet potato, peeled and diced

1 tablespoon melted margarine

1 Vidalia onion, finely chopped

1 tablespoon balsamic vinegar

1/2 teaspoon paprika

1/4 teaspoon sea salt

1/4 teaspoon ground black pepper

Directions

Firstly, treat sweet potatoes with melted margarine.

Then, in a mixing dish, combine other ingredients; stir until thoroughly combined.

Air-fry sweet potatoes at 375 degrees F for 25 minutes or until they are softened; make sure to turn them occasionally.

Taste, adjust the seasonings and eat warm. Bon appétit!

199. Dijon Roasted Potatoes

(Ready in about 25 minutes | Servings 4)

Ingredients

4 large-sized red potatoes, quartered

Nonstick cooking spray

1 tablespoon Dijon mustard

1 fresh sprig rosemary, chopped

2 fresh sprigs thyme, chopped

1 teaspoon shallot powder

1/2 teaspoon garlic powder

Sea salt and cayenne pepper, to taste

Directions

Blot the cut-side of potatoes with a paper towel in order to remove any excess moisture. Brush them with a nonstick cooking spray.

In a bowl, mix together Dijon mustard, rosemary, thyme, shallot powder, and garlic powder. Rub the potatoes with Dijon mixture.

Season the potatoes with salt and cayenne pepper; now, roast them for 25 minutes at 375 degrees F. Turn them a few times during the cooking process. Eat warm. Bon appétit!

200. Summer Wonton Cups

(Ready in about 10 minutes | Servings 6)

Ingredients

1/4 cup cream cheese

1/2 cup mayonnaise

1 (6-ounce) can crabmeat, drained

1 teaspoon dried rosemary, crushed

Salt and ground black pepper, to taste

20 wonton wrappers

1 cup Swiss cheese, shredded

Roughly chopped fresh parsley, for garnish

Directions

In a mixing dish, thoroughly combine cream cheese, mayonnaise, and crabmeat.

Now, season with rosemary, salt, and ground black pepper. Stir to combine well.

Now, place 1 wonton wrapper in each mini muffin cup. Then, divide the mixture among cups. Top with shredded Swiss cheese.

Bake at 330 degrees F for 10 minutes. Garnish with fresh parsley and serve. Bon appétit!

201. Honey and Cinnamon Sweet Potatoes

(Ready in about 25 minutes | Servings 4)

Ingredients

4 cups sweet potato, peeled and diced

1 tablespoon butter, melted

1/2 cup honey

2 tablespoons ground cinnamon

A pinch of salt

A pinch of ground black pepper

1/4 teaspoon grated nutmeg

Directions

Toss all ingredients in a mixing dish.

Air-fry sweet potatoes at 375 degrees F for 25 minutes or until they are browned; pause the machine and shake them occasionally.

Taste, adjust the seasonings and serve. Bon appétit!

202. Parmesan Cheese Sticks

(Ready in about 10 minutes | Servings 6)

Ingredients

2 eggs, beaten

Salt and ground black pepper, to your liking

2 cups cracker crumbs

1/2 cup Parmesan cheese, grated

1/2 cup flour

12 sticks string cheese

Nonstick cooking spray

Directions

Whisk the eggs, along with the salt and black pepper in a mixing bowl. In a separate bowl, mix the crumbs together with the Parmesan cheese.

Place the flour in the third bowl. Coat the sticks with the flour. Then, dip them in the egg mixture; afterward, dip each stick in the Parmesan mixture. Brush each stick with a nonstick cooking spray.

Air-fry the sticks in a single layer at 400 degrees F for about 8 minutes, turning over halfway through. Serve with a dipping sauce of choice.

203. Roasted Tomato and Mozzarella Bites

(Ready in about 20 minutes | Servings 6)

Ingredients

4 large tomatoes, quartered

2 tablespoons extra-virgin olive oil

1 tablespoon apple cider vinegar

Sea salt and ground black pepper, to taste

1/2 teaspoon cayenne pepper

16 small balls fresh mozzarella cheese

1 heaping tablespoon fresh rosemary, roughly chopped

Directions

Place your tomatoes on a baking sheet, cut side up.

Drizzle the oil and vinegar over the tomatoes, sprinkle them with the salt, black pepper, and cayenne pepper.

Roast them at 330 degrees F for about 15 minutes, working with batches. Now, pause the machine and top each tomato with the mozzarella ball. Air-fry for another 5 minutes.

Scatter chopped rosemary over the roasted tomatoes and serve at room temperature.

204. The Best Corn Dip Ever

(Ready in about 15 minutes | Servings 10)

Ingredients

1 tablespoon butter

1 tablespoon flour

1/2 cup half-and-half

Sea salt and freshly ground black pepper, to taste

10 ounces frozen corn kernels

1/2 cup Romano cheese, grated

Directions

Thoroughly combine all ingredients in a mixing bowl.

Scrape the mixture into a baking dish; air-fry for 15 minutes at 330 degrees F. Serve with tortilla chips or breadsticks. Enjoy!

205. Scallion and Pepper Corn Bites

(Ready in about 15 minutes | Servings 8)

Ingredients

1 cup cornmeal

1/2 cup flour

1 teaspoon baking powder

1 teaspoon baking soda

A pinch of salt

1/4 teaspoon ground black pepper

1 red bell pepper, seeded and finely chopped

1 green bell pepper, seeded and finely chopped

1/2 cup scallions, finely chopped

1/3 cup milk

2 eggs, beaten

2 tablespoons butter, melted

Directions

In a mixing bowl, combine the cornmeal, flour, baking powder, baking soda, salt, and black pepper.

In another bowl, combine together the remaining ingredients. Fold the pepper/scallion mixture into the cornmeal mixture; mix to combine well.

Then, grease a mini muffin pan with a nonstick cooking spray.

Divide the batter among prepared mini muffin cups. Bake for 10 minutes at 330 degrees F, working in batches as needed. Enjoy!

206. Shrimp Wonton Cups

(Ready in about 10 minutes | Servings 6)

Ingredients

3/4 cup shrimp, patted dry and chopped

1/3 cup sweet chili sauce

1/4 cup soft cheese

1 teaspoon Dijon mustard

1/2 teaspoon dried oregano

1/2 teaspoon dried basil, crushed

Sea salt and ground black pepper, to taste

20 wonton wrappers

1 cup yellow cheese, shredded

Black sesame seeds, for garnish

Directions

In a mixing dish, thoroughly combine the shrimp, chili sauce, soft cheese, and mustard.

Next, stir in oregano, basil, salt, and black pepper and stir well.

Add 1 wonton wrapper to each mini-muffin cup and press gently. Then, divide the mixture among cups. Top with shredded yellow cheese.

Bake at 330 degrees F for 10 minutes. Garnish with sesame seeds and serve.

207. Hot Cheese Sticks

(Ready in about 10 minutes | Servings 4)

Ingredients

1/2 teaspoon red chili powder

2 cups seasoned bread crumbs

1/4 cup all-purpose flour

1/4 cup corn flour

Salt and cayenne pepper, to your liking

8 thick cheese slices

Nonstick cooking spray

Directions

In a mixing bowl, combine chili powder, 1 cup of bread crumbs, all-purpose flour, and corn flour. Add water, little by little, in order to make a thick batter.

In another bowl, add the remaining 1 cup of bread crumbs; add the salt and cayenne pepper, and stir to combine well.

Roll the cheese slices in the batter; make sure to coat them well. Now, dredge them in the breadcrumb mixture.

Brush the cheese sticks with a nonstick cooking spray. Air-fry the sticks at 400 degrees F for about 8 minutes, turning over halfway through. Serve hot with salsa, if desired.

208. Zesty Sweet Potato Fries

(Ready in about 20 minutes | Servings 4)

Ingredients

4 sweet potatoes, peeled and diced

1 tablespoon coconut oil

1/2 cup Italian salad dressing

1/4 cup grated Parmesan cheese

Kosher salt and ground black pepper, to taste

Directions

Toss all ingredients in a mixing dish.

Cook the fries at 375 degrees F for 20 minutes; pause the machine to shake them periodically. Bon appétit!

209. Amazing Cheddar and Pea Dip

(Ready in about 15 minutes | Servings 10)

Ingredients

1 tablespoon flour

2 tablespoons mayonnaise

1 tablespoon butter

1/2 cup half-and-half

Sea salt and freshly ground black pepper, to taste

1 teaspoon red pepper flakes, crushed

10 ounces frozen green peas

1/2 cup Cheddar cheese, grated

Directions

Add all of the above ingredients to a mixing bowl.

Scrape the mixture into a baking dish; bake for 15 minutes at 330 degrees F. Serve with dippers of choice.

210. BBQ Potato Snack

(Ready in about 40 minutes | Servings 8)

Ingredients

4 medium-sized potatoes, thinly sliced

Nonstick cooking spray

1 tablespoon shallot powder

1 teaspoon garlic powder

1 teaspoon brown sugar

1/2 teaspoon chili powder

Sea salt, to taste

Directions

Firstly, soak the potato slices in the cold water for 30 minutes.

Place the potatoes on a kitchen towel and dry them. Rub them with a cooking spray on all sides.

Bake in an air fryer basket at 400 degrees F for 5 minutes. Pause the machine and toss. Bake for another 5 minutes or until they're crisp. Work with batches.

Meanwhile, in a large freezer bag, combine all seasonings. Toss prepared chips with the spice mixture. Serve with dipping sauce, if desired.

211. Easy Jalapeño Wontons

(Ready in about 10 minutes | Servings 6)

Ingredients

8 ounces Cottage cheese, room temperature

2 jalapeño peppers, finely chopped

1/2 cup Colby cheese, shredded

1/2 teaspoon salt

1/4 teaspoon ground black pepper

1/2 teaspoon cayenne pepper

1 teaspoon dried rosemary, finely minced

1 teaspoon garlic, finely minced

24 square wonton wrappers

Nonstick cooking spray

Directions

In a mixing bowl, combine Cottage cheese, jalapeños, Colby cheese, salt, black pepper, cayenne pepper, rosemary, and garlic.

Place one wonton in each muffin cup. Add the cheese mixture to the cups. Place them on the fryer rack; brush them with the cooking oil.

Fry at 350 degrees F for about 10 minutes. Bon appétit!

212. Crispy Artichoke Hearts

(Ready in about 10 minutes | Servings 6)

Ingredients

1 (15-ounce) can artichoke hearts in water

1 teaspoon fresh lemon juice

Salt and black pepper, to your liking

2 eggs

1 cup Italian seasoned breadcrumbs

1/4 cup Romano cheese, grated

2 tablespoons roughly chopped flat-leaf parsley

Directions

Drain the artichokes and cut them into wedges. Drizzle fresh lemon juice over them; add the salt and black pepper

In a shallow bowl, whisk the eggs. In another bowl, add the breadcrumbs and Romano cheese; mix well to combine.

Dip your artichokes in the eggs; then coat them with the breadcrumb mixture. Then, spray your artichokes on all sides with canola oil.

Place the artichokes in a single layer in the cooking basket; bake at 400 degrees F for 10 minutes, turning halfway through. Sprinkle with fresh parsley and serve at room temperature.

213. Roasted Carrots with Coriander

(Ready in about 20 minutes | Servings 4)

Ingredients

1 pound carrots, trimmed

1 tablespoon sesame oil

1 teaspoon sunflower seeds

1 tablespoon honey

1 handful of fresh coriander

Directions

Drizzle the carrots with the sesame oil. Add the sunflower seeds and honey; toss to coat well.

Roast the carrot at 390 degrees F for about 20 minutes, or until tender.

Transfer the carrots to a nice serving platter. Scatter fresh coriander over the carrots and serve.

214. Fall Sweet Potato Fries

(Ready in about 30 minutes | Servings 8)

Ingredients

2 pound sweet potatoes, peeled and cut into wedges

2 tablespoons vegetable oil

1 tablespoon brown sugar

1 teaspoon kosher salt

1 tablespoon pumpkin pie spice

1 tablespoon chipotle powder

Directions

Firstly, microwave sweet potatoes for 3 minutes on HIGH. After that, allow them to cool slightly.

Toss sweet potatoes with the remaining items. Coat sweet potatoes well.

Bake at 400 degrees F for 25 minutes, turning halfway through. Serve with mayo and ketchup for dipping, if desired. Enjoy!

215. Delicious Carrot Chips

(Ready in about 10 minutes | Servings 4)

Ingredients

4 medium carrots, peeled and thinly sliced

1 tablespoon olive oil

A pinch of grated nutmeg

1/2 teaspoon ground cinnamon

A pinch of kosher salt

Directions

In a large bowl, toss the carrot with other ingredients.

Next, lay the slices out in an air fryer basket. Bake at 400 degrees F for 5 minutes, working in batches.

Pause the machine, open and toss the ingredients. Bake for another 5 minutes or until the carrot slices are crisp.

216. Garlic and Cilantro Mushroom Appetizer

(Ready in about 10 minutes | Servings 6)

Ingredients

2 slices stale bread, grind into crumbs

2 cloves garlic, finely minced

1 tablespoon fresh cilantro, chopped

Sea salt and ground black pepper, to taste

2 tablespoons olive oil

24 mushrooms cups

Directions

Mix the breadcrumbs with the garlic, cilantro, sea salt, and ground black pepper. Now, add the olive oil and mix again.

Then, fill the mushroom caps with the breadcrumb/garlic mixture. Transfer the mushrooms to the air fryer basket.

Fry at 390 degrees F for 10 minutes or until golden. Bon appétit!

217. Rosemary Zucchini Fries

(Ready in about 15 minutes | Servings 6)

Ingredients

1/2 cup seasoned breadcrumbs

1/4 cup Parmigiano-Reggiano cheese, grated

1/2 teaspoon dried oregano

1 teaspoon rosemary

1/2 teaspoon smoked cayenne pepper

2 egg whites, whisked

2 zucchinis, cut into wedges

Salt and ground black pepper, to taste

Canola oil

Fresh chopped rosemary, for garnish

Directions

In a bowl, combine together the breadcrumbs, Parmigiano-Reggiano, oregano, rosemary, and smoked cayenne pepper. Reserve.

Add the whisked egg whites to a shallow bowl.

Season zucchini with salt and black pepper. Dip each zucchini wedge in the egg whites. Then, coat them with the breadcrumb mixture. Place the wedges in a single layer in an air fryer pan.

Spray them with canola oil on all sides. Air-fry at 350 degrees F for 7 minutes, working in batches. Turn them over and fry for 7 more minutes. Serve sprinkled with some extra rosemary if desired.

218. Paprika Zucchini Chips

(Ready in about 10 minutes | Servings 6)

Ingredients

2 medium zucchinis, peeled and thinly sliced

1 tablespoon canola oil

1 teaspoon hot smoked paprika

A pinch of kosher salt

Directions

In a large-sized mixing bowl, toss the zucchini slices with other ingredients.

Then, lay the slices out in an air fryer basket. Bake at 400 degrees F for 5 minutes, working in batches.

Pause the machine, open and toss the ingredients. Bake for another 5 minutes or till the zucchini slices are crisp. Eat immediately or store in an air-tight container.

219. Tangy Sweet Potato Fries

(Ready in about 30 minutes | Servings 8)

Ingredients

2 pounds sweet potatoes, peeled and cut into wedges

2 tablespoons canola oil

1 teaspoon lime zest, grated

1 tablespoon agave nectar

1 teaspoon paprika

1 teaspoon kosher salt

1 tablespoon Cajun spice mix

Directions

Microwave sweet potatoes for 3 minutes on HIGH. Allow them to cool slightly.

Toss sweet potatoes with the other ingredients. Toss to coat well.

Bake at 400 degrees F for 25 minutes or till they're golden brown on all sides, turning `halfway through. Serve with favorite sauce for dipping.

DINNER

220. Mexican-Style Bean Burgers

(Ready in about 20 minutes | Servings 4)

Ingredients

1 (16-ounce) can kidney beans

1 small red bell pepper, diced

1/2 cup red onions, finely chopped

1 tablespoon mild chili powder

2 cloves garlic, minced

1 egg, well-beaten

Sea salt and ground black pepper, to taste

1 tablespoon cumin powder

2 tablespoons salsa

1/2 cup tortilla chips, crushed

Directions

Empty the can with beans into the mixing bowl; then, mash your beans using a potato masher.

Add the remaining ingredients and mix to combine. Shape the mixture into four patties.

Cook bean burgers in the air fryer at 390 degrees F for 15 to 18 minutes.

To serve: Split the burger buns in half and add the burgers. Top with avocado slices and some extra salsa if desired. Enjoy!

221. Crispy Coconut Shrimp

(Ready in about 10 minutes | Servings 4)

Ingredients

1/2 cup all-purpose flour

1/4 teaspoon ground black pepper

1/2 teaspoon salt

1/4 teaspoon paprika

2 egg whites

1/2 cup breadcrumbs

1/2 cup unsweetened coconut, shredded

Zest of 1 lemon

20 large-sized shrimp, peeled and de-veined

Nonstick cooking spray

Chili sauce, for serving

Directions

Place the flour along with black pepper, salt, and paprika in a shallow dish. Whisk the eggs whites in the second shallow dish.

In the third dish, combine the breadcrumbs, coconut, and lemon zest.

Then, preheat your air fryer to 400 degrees F. Now, dredge your shrimp in the flour mixture; now, dip it in the whisked egg white. Lastly, press it into the breadcrumb mixture. Just make sure to coat all sides.

Brush the breaded shrimp with cooking oil. Cook for about 6 minutes. Work with batches.

Decrease the temperature to 340 degrees F. Cook all batches another 2 minutes. Serve with chili sauce.

222. Pepper and Scallion Pizza

(Ready in about 20 minutes | Servings 4)

Ingredients

4 ounces prepared pizza dough

1 tablespoon olive oil

1 red bell pepper, seeded and chopped

1 green bell pepper, seeded and chopped

1 cup scallions, chopped

3/4 teaspoon dried oregano, crushed

1/2 teaspoon dried basil, crushed

1 teaspoon cayenne pepper

Sea salt and ground black pepper, to your liking

1/2 cup Colby cheese, shredded

Directions

Roll the pizza dough out. Add the dough to the tray; brush it with a cooking spray. Bake it at 350 degrees F for 5 minutes.

Turn the dough over, brush with the cooking spray again, and bake an additional 5 minutes. Reserve.

Grease an ovenproof dish with 1 tablespoon of olive oil. Add bell peppers and scallions to the ovenproof dish.

Sprinkle with the oregano, basil, cayenne pepper, salt, and ground black pepper. Air fry at 400 degrees F for 5 minutes or until tender.

Spread the pepper/scallion mixture over the prepared pizza crust, top with the Colby cheese. Return to your air fryer and bake for 5 more minutes at 400 degrees F. Enjoy!

223. Sunday Halibut Steak

(Ready in about 45 minutes | Servings 4)

Ingredients

1 pound halibut steak

1/2 cup dry white wine

2/3 cup soy sauce

1/4 cup sugar

1/4 cup of orange juice

1/4 black pepper, preferably freshly ground

1/2 teaspoon sea salt

1/2 teaspoon shallot powder

1 teaspoon mustard seeds

1/4 teaspoon ground ginger

Directions

Prepare your marinade by mixing all ingredients, except for halibut. Now, boil the mixture in a sauté pan until reduced by half. Allow it to cool fully.

Put half of the cooled marinade in a resealable bag. Place halibut steak in the marinade for about 30 minutes in the refrigerator.

Preheat your air fryer to a temperature of 390 degrees F. Air-fry the halibut steaks for 10 to 12 minutes.

Lastly, brush the halibut steak with the remaining marinate. Serve over boiled potatoes.

224. Dilled Saucy Salmon

(Ready in about 15 minutes | Servings 4)

Ingredients

4 pieces of salmon

1 tablespoon extra-virgin olive oil

1/4 teaspoon seasoned salt

1/2 teaspoon ground black pepper

1/2 teaspoon paprika

1/2 teaspoon dried thyme

2 tablespoons mayonnaise

1/4 cup Greek yogurt

1/2 cup sour cream

2 tablespoons fresh dill, finely chopped

Directions

Preheat your air fryer to 270 degrees F.

Drizzle olive oil over your fish. Add all seasonings, making sure to coat salmon well.

Transfer the salmon pieces to the food basket.

While the fish is frying, prepare the sauce by mixing all remaining ingredients. Serve and garnish with the sauce.

225. Perfect Creamy Potatoes

(Ready in about 35 minutes | Servings 4)

Ingredients

8 russet potatoes, peeled and sliced

1 teaspoon sea salt

1/2 teaspoon ground black pepper

1/2 cup cream

1/2 cup milk

1/2 teaspoon freshly grated nutmeg

1 teaspoon cayenne pepper

Blue cheese, to serve

Directions

Place the potatoes in a bowl, followed by salt and black pepper. In another mixing bowl, whisk together the cream, milk, nutmeg, and cayenne pepper.

Add the cream mixture to the potato mixture and gently stir to coat well.

Then, arrange the potato slices evenly in a baking dish. Pour the cream mixture over the potatoes. Cook for 25 minutes at 340 degrees F, or until it is done.

Cover prepared potatoes with blue cheese. Add the food basket back to the air fryer; let it cook an additional 10 minutes or till blue cheese has melted.

226. Light and Easy Cod Fillets

(Ready in about 15 minutes | Servings 4)

Ingredients

2 tablespoons canola oil

1 cup breadcrumbs

Salt and ground black pepper

1 egg, whisked

4 pieces of cod fillets

1 lemon, sliced into wedges

Directions

Set your air fryer to 360 degrees F. Combine canola oil, breadcrumbs, salt, and ground black pepper in a mixing bowl; stir until the mixture forms loose crumbs.

In another bowl, beat the egg. Dip fish fillet in the beaten egg. Coat the fillets with the breadcrumb mixture.

Place the coated fillets in a single layer in the food basket. Fry them for 12 minutes, working in batches. Serve the cod fillets with lemon wedges. Enjoy!

227. Tomato and Cheese Dinner

(Ready in about 15 minutes | Servings 4)

Ingredients

For the Pesto:

1/2 cup fresh basil leaves, roughly chopped

1/4 cup fresh cilantro, roughly chopped

1/2 cup Parmesan cheese, grated

2 cloves garlic, toasted and smashed

1/2 teaspoon salt

1/4 cup extra-virgin olive oil

For the Tomatoes and Feta:

2 medium-sized tomatoes, thinly sliced

8 ounces feta cheese, thinly sliced

1/2 cup scallions, chopped

1 tablespoon extra-virgin olive oil

Directions

Make pesto by mixing all ingredients in a food processor, except the olive oil. While the machine is running, add olive oil in a thin stream. Set aside.

Preheat the air fryer to 390 degrees F.

Next, spread an even layer of pesto on top of each tomato slice. Top with feta cheese and scallions. Drizzle olive oil over all.

Arrange prepared tomato and feta in the food basket. Cook for about 14 minutes.

228. Mac and Cheese with Broccoli

(Ready in about 15 minutes | Servings 4)

Ingredients

1 cup macaroni

1/2 cup broccoli, cut into small-sized florets

1/2 cup warmed milk

1 ½ cups Gruyere cheese, grated

1/4 teaspoon ground black pepper

1/2 teaspoon red pepper flakes, crushed

1/2 teaspoon sea salt

Parmesan cheese, to garnish

Directions

Begin by preheating the air fryer to 400 degrees F.

Then, bring a pot of lightly salted water to a rapid boil over high heat; after that, lower the heat to medium. Cook macaroni and broccoli.

Simmer until your pasta is al dente. Drain pasta and broccoli; add them back to the pot. Add the milk and Gruyere cheese; toss to combine. Season with black pepper, red pepper, and salt.

Scrape the mixture into an ovenproof dish. Sprinkle the Parmesan cheese over the top. Transfer the dish to the air fryer basket and adjust the temperature to 350 degrees F; bake for 15 minutes. Enjoy!

229. Restaurant-Style Cheeseburgers

(Ready in about 45 minutes | Servings 4)

Ingredients

1/2 pound ground beef

1 yellow onion, chopped

2 cloves garlic, peeled and smashed

1 tablespoon tomato puree

1 teaspoon dried basil

1 teaspoon dried oregano

1/2 teaspoon dried rosemary

Salt and ground black pepper, to your liking

4 slices of yellow cheese

4 bread buns

Topping of choice, to serve

Directions

In a mixing dish, combine the ground meat, onion, garlic, tomato puree, and all seasoning; mix well to combine.

Form the mixture into 4 equal burgers; arrange them on the air fryer cooking tray.

Cook them at 400 degrees F for 25 minutes; now, lower the temperature to 350 degrees F and cook them for further 20 minutes.

Assemble the sandwiches with buns yellow cheese, burger buns, and a topping of choice. Enjoy!

230. Simple Parsley Fries

(Ready in about 25 minutes | Servings 4)

Ingredients

4 potatoes, peeled and cut into fries

4 tablespoons olive oil

1/2 teaspoon salt

1/4 teaspoon ground black pepper

1 tablespoon fresh parsley, finely chopped

Directions

Place the potatoes in your air fryer; add the olive oil. Season with salt, pepper, and parsley.

Fry at 350 degrees F for 2 minutes; now, shake them and cook for a further 8 minutes.

Then, shake again, and fry for a further 15 minutes. Serve and enjoy!

231. Seasoned Air Fried Chips

(Ready in about 25 minutes | Servings 4)

Ingredients

1 pound Idaho potatoes, peeled and cut into fries

4 tablespoons canola oil

2 tablespoons dried ancho chili powder

1 tablespoon salt

2 teaspoons ground cumin

Directions

Place all ingredients in the air fryer basket.

Fry at 350 degrees F for 2 minutes; now, shake them and air-fry for 8 more minutes.

Shake again and air-fry for an additional 15 minutes. Bon appétit!

232. Herbed Jacket Potatoes

(Ready in about 15 minutes | Servings 4)

Ingredients

4 potatoes

2 tablespoons olive oil

1/2 cup sour cream

1/2 cup Colby cheese, grated

1 teaspoon dried thyme

1/2 teaspoon dried rosemary

1/2 teaspoon celery seeds

Sea salt and ground black pepper, to taste

Directions

Prick the potatoes with a fork and air-fry them at 350 degrees F for 15 minutes.

Meanwhile, prepare the filling by mixing together all remaining ingredients.

When the potatoes are cooked, open them up and spread with the filling mixture. Serve right away.

233. Easiest Chicken Nuggets Ever

(Ready in about 15 minutes | Servings 4)

Ingredients

1/4 cup seasoned breadcrumbs

1/2 teaspoon cayenne pepper

Salt and ground black pepper, to taste

1 tablespoon olive oil

1/2 pound chicken breast, minced

1 tablespoon tomato puree

2 eggs, beaten

1 teaspoon dried thyme

1 teaspoon dried marjoram

Directions

Mix the breadcrumbs with the cayenne pepper, salt and black pepper. Now, add the olive oil and mix to combine.

Combine minced chicken breast with the tomato puree, 1 egg, thyme, and marjoram. Add the second beaten egg to a shallow bowl.

Form the chicken mixture into chicken nugget shapes; now, coat them with the egg; then, dredge them in the breadcrumbs.

Cook for 10 minutes at 400 degrees F. Serve and enjoy!

234. Spring Stuffed Mushrooms

(Ready in about 15 minutes | Servings 3)

Ingredients

1/2 cup green onions, chopped

1 tablespoon crushed bran cereal

1 teaspoon garlic puree

1 tablespoon canola oil

6 mushrooms

Salt and freshly cracked black pepper, to your liking

Directions

In a mixing dish, combine together green onions, crushed bran cereal, and garlic puree. Stir until they are well mixed.

To make the "shells", remove the middle stalks from your mushrooms. Fill the mushrooms with green onion mixture. Drizzle canola oil over them.

Air-fry the mushrooms at 350 degrees F for 10 to 12 minutes. Season with salt and black pepper and serve warm.

235. Jumbo Prawns with Mayo-Honey Sauce

(Ready in about 10 minutes | Servings 4)

Ingredients

4 jumbo prawns

1/4 teaspoon smoked paprika

1 teaspoon salt

1/4 teaspoon ground black pepper

3 egg whites

2 tablespoons rice flour

4 tablespoons mayonnaise

1 tablespoon honey

1 tablespoon milk

Directions

Season the prawns with smoked paprika, salt, and black pepper.

Whip egg whites until foamy; add rice flour and stir to combine well. Dip each prawn into the batter.

Next, fry your prawns at 350 degrees F for 8 minutes.

In the meantime, prepare the sauce by mixing mayonnaise, honey, and milk.

Serve fried prawns with the mayo sauce and enjoy!

236. Air Fryer Fish Fillets

(Ready in about 15 minutes | Servings 4)

Ingredients

1 tablespoon fresh lemon juice

4 small-sized fish fillets

6-7 crackers

1/4 cup tortilla chips

1 egg, well beaten

Salt and ground black pepper

Directions

Drizzle fresh lemon juice over the fish fillets.

In your food processor, grind the crackers and tortilla chips. Cover the fish with the egg; then, coat it with cracker mixture. Season with salt and pepper.

Fry your fish for 15 minutes at 350 degrees F. Serve with chips and enjoy!

237. Onion and Sausage Balls with French Fries

(Ready in about 40 minutes | Servings 4)

Ingredients

For the Balls:

1 cup sausage meat

1 small-sized onion, diced

3/4 teaspoon garlic puree

3 tablespoons breadcrumbs

1/2 teaspoon seasoned salt

Freshly ground black pepper, to your liking

For the Fries:

1 pound Idaho potatoes, peeled and cut into fries

4 tablespoons olive oil

1 teaspoon onion powder

1 tablespoon salt

Directions

Place all ingredients for the balls in a mixing dish; mix with your hands until everything is well incorporated. Form the mixture into the balls.

Cook the balls in your air fryer at 350 degrees F for 15 minutes. Set the balls aside, keeping them warm.

Then, put all ingredients for the fries into the air fryer basket. Air-fry at 350 degrees F for 25 minutes, shaking them a few times.

Serve onion balls with French fries. Bon appétit!

238. Herbes de Provence Fries

(Ready in about 25 minutes | Servings 4)

Ingredients

4 potatoes, peeled and cut into fries

4 tablespoons olive oil

1 teaspoon lemon juice

2 tablespoons herbes de Provence

1/2 teaspoon smoked paprika

1 tablespoon salt

Directions

Place all ingredients in the air fryer basket.

Working in batches, fry the potatoes at 350 degrees F for 25 minutes. Make sure to shake the fries a few times.

Serve warm with tomato ketchup and mayonnaise. Bon appétit!

239. Garlic Chicken Breasts with Mushrooms

(Ready in about 35 minutes | Servings 6)

Ingredients

4 medium-sized chicken breasts, sliced

1/4 teaspoon smoked paprika

Salt and ground black pepper, to your liking

3/4 pound mushrooms, thinly sliced

2 tablespoons flour

2 tablespoons canola oil

4 cloves garlic, minced

1/4 cup pear cider vinegar

1 cup chicken stock

1/4 teaspoon dried rosemary

Directions

Season the breasts with paprika, salt, and black pepper.

Layer the seasoned chicken in the baking dish. Transfer the dish to the air fryer and cook for 20 minutes at 350 degrees F.

Then, pause your air fryer and throw in the mushrooms, followed by the other ingredients. Cook for another 12 minutes.

Serve with a side salad and enjoy!

240. Easy Pork Sandwiches

(Ready in about 4 hours + 30 minutes | Servings 4)

Ingredients

14 ounces canned cream of celery soup

3 pounds boneless pork ribs

Barbeque sauce of choice

Salt and black pepper, to taste

Directions

Pour the canned soup into your slow cooker; add the pork. Cook on HIGH heat for 4 hours.

Then, shred the meat with two forks. Preheat your air fryer to 350 degrees F.

Next, add the pork to a baking dish; stir in the barbeque sauce. Season with salt and pepper to taste. Cook for 30 minutes in your air fryer and serve with hamburger buns.

241. Country-Style Beef Patties

(Ready in about 15 minutes | Servings 4)

Ingredients

1/2 pound ground beef

1/2 pound ground pork

1 tablespoon Worcestershire sauce

1/2 teaspoon shallot powder

1/4 teaspoon ground black pepper

1/4 teaspoon cayenne pepper

1/2 teaspoon sea salt

1/2 teaspoon dried basil

Directions

In a small-sized bowl, mix all of the above ingredients. Now, shape the mixture into 4 patties.

Preheat your air fryer to 390 degrees F. Transfer the patties to the baking pan; cook for 12 minutes. Serve on hamburger buns.

242. Broccoli with Peppers and Mushrooms

(Ready in about 35 minutes | Servings 4)

Ingredients

1 head broccoli, broken into florets

2 tablespoons olive oil

2 tablespoons Oyster sauce

2 bell pepper, trimmed and chopped

3 cloves garlic, finely minced

1 teaspoon fresh ginger, grated

Salt and ground black pepper, to taste

1/2 teaspoon paprika

2 pounds canned mushrooms, sliced

Directions

Add all of the above ingredients, except for canned mushrooms, to the air fryer basket. Cook at 375 degrees F for 20 minutes, working with batches.

Toss in the mushrooms and let it cook for another 15 minutes. Bon appétit!

243. Cheesy Chicken Meatloaf

(Ready in about 45 minutes | Servings 8)

Ingredients

2 pounds ground chicken

1 cup milk

1 cup mixed breadcrumbs and crumbled tortilla chips

2 whole eggs

4 gloves garlic, peeled and minced

1/2 cup fresh flat-leaf parsley, chopped

1 teaspoon Dijon mustard

Salt and ground black pepper, to taste

3/4 pound Cheddar cheese, diced

1/2 cup tomato ketchup

Directions

Start by preheating your air fryer to 390 degrees F.

In a bowl, mix all ingredients, except tomato ketchup. Transfer the mixture to the loaf pan and top with ketchup.

Place the pan in your air fryer; cook for 45 minutes. Bon appétit!

244. Chinese-Style Pork Ribs

(Ready in about 1 hour 25 minutes | Servings 4)

Ingredients

1 rack of pork ribs

1 tablespoon water

1 tablespoon soy sauce

1/2 teaspoon ground black pepper

1/2 teaspoon sea salt

1 tablespoon cornstarch

1/2 teaspoon vegetable oil

1 teaspoon Five spice powder

Directions

Start by preheating your air fryer to 390 degrees F. Now, place the ribs in a bowl.

Add the other ingredients and toss to coat evenly. Now, marinate the ribs for about 1 hour.

After that, cook the marinated ribs approximately 25 minutes. Serve warm and enjoy!

245. Parmesan and Chipotle Chicken

(Ready in about 25 minutes | Servings 4)

Ingredients

1 cup breadcrumbs

1/4 cup Parmesan cheese, shredded

1/4 teaspoon cayenne pepper

1/2 teaspoon ground black pepper, or to taste

1/2 teaspoon seasoned salt

2 tablespoons sour cream

1/2 cup mayonnaise

2 chipotle chilies in adobo sauce

2 chicken breasts, halved

Directions

In a medium bowl, mix the breadcrumbs, Parmesan, cayenne pepper, black pepper, and salt.

In a food processor, combine the sour cream, mayonnaise and chipotle chilies; process until there are no lumps.

Coat the chicken breasts with the mayo mixture. Dip chicken breasts in the breadcrumb mixture.

Preheat the air fryer to 350 degrees F. Then, cook for about 25 minutes. Serve and enjoy!

246. Grandma's Famous Beef Chili

(Ready in about 35 minutes | Servings 6)

Ingredients

1 tablespoon olive oil

2 cloves garlic, minced

1 onion, finely chopped

1/2 cup celery, diced

1/2 cup green bell pepper, diced

1 pound ground beef

1 ½ cups vegetable broth

1 teaspoon coriander

1/2 tablespoon chili powder

1/2 teaspoon dried parsley

1 can tomatoes, diced

1 (15-ounce) can cannellini beans with liquid

1/4 teaspoon hot pepper sauce

1 teaspoon kosher salt

1/4 teaspoon ground black pepper, or to taste

Directions

Place the oil, garlic, onion, celery and bell pepper in the air fryer baking dish. Cook for 5 minutes at 350 degrees F.

Add the beef and cook for 6 minutes longer. Add the broth, coriander, chili powder, dried parsley, and tomatoes. Cook for 20 minutes longer.

Throw in the beans; add hot pepper sauce, salt, and ground black pepper; let it cook an additional 10 minutes. Serve warm.

247. Garam Masala Tilapia Fillets

(Ready in about 20 minutes | Servings 4)

Ingredients

Nonstick cooking spray

4 tilapia fillets

1/2 teaspoon sea salt

1/4 teaspoon ground black pepper

1/2 teaspoon cayenne pepper

1/2 cup coconut milk

1/2 cup coriander

1 teaspoon grated ginger

1 teaspoon Garam masala

3 garlic cloves, minced

Directions

Preheat your air fryer to 390 degrees F. Lightly grease the baking dish with a nonstick cooking spray. Season the tilapia fillets with the salt, black pepper, cayenne pepper; place them in the baking dish.

In a food processor, pulse the other ingredients until it forms a smooth consistency. Coat the tilapia with this mixture.

Now, cook your fish for about 14 minutes. Serve over rice.

248. Coconut Curried Prawns

(Ready in about 10 minutes | Servings 4)

Ingredients

4 jumbo prawns

1 cup desiccated coconut

1/2 teaspoon garlic paste

1 teaspoon seasoned salt

1/4 teaspoon ground black pepper

1 tablespoon curry leaf, finely chopped

1/2 cup fresh lemon juice

1 teaspoon chili powder

2 tablespoons flour

1 egg, beaten

Directions

In a mixing bowl, combine all ingredients, except for prawns and coconut.

Dip the prawns in the marinade. Then, coat marinated prawns with coconut.

Fry your prawns at 350 degrees F for 8 minutes. Serve with sauce and enjoy!

249. Coconut Chicken Drumsticks

(Ready in about 25 minutes | Servings 4)

Ingredients

4 chicken drumsticks

1/2 cup coconut milk

2 tablespoons ground turmeric

3 tablespoons ginger, minced

1/2 teaspoon sea salt

Directions

Prepare the marinade by mixing all ingredients, except the chicken drumsticks. Now, mix the ingredients thoroughly.

Next, marinate chicken drumsticks overnight in your refrigerator.

Cook the chicken at 375 degrees F for 25 minutes; make sure to flip them over at half-time. Serve with salad and enjoy!

250. Nana's Spaghetti Bolognaise

(Ready in about 30 minutes | Servings 4)

Ingredients

3/4 pound ground beef

1 bell pepper, seeded and chopped

1 stalk of celery, finely chopped

1 can chopped tomatoes

2 cloves garlic, finely minced

1/2 teaspoon ground black pepper

1/2 teaspoon seasoned salt

Cayenne pepper to taste

1 box spaghetti

Directions

Place the ground beef in an oven safe bowl and cook for 12 minutes at 390 degrees F.

Stir in the other ingredients, except for spaghetti, and cook for another 18 minutes. Serve over cooked pasta and enjoy!

251. White Bean Burgers

(Ready in about 18 minutes | Servings 4)

Ingredients

1 (16-ounce) can white beans

1 small red bell pepper, diced

1/2 cup scallions, chopped

2 cloves garlic, minced

1 egg, well-beaten

Sea salt and ground black pepper, to taste

1 tablespoon cumin powder

1 tablespoon soy sauce

1/2 cup tortilla chips, crushed

Directions

Mash the beans until they form a thick paste.

Throw in the remaining ingredients; mix to combine well. Shape the mixture into 4 veggie patties.

Cook your burgers in the air fryer at 390 degrees F for 15 to 18 minutes or until crispy.

252. Finger-Lickin' Barbecued Ribs

(Ready in about 25 minutes | Servings 4)

Ingredients

1 pound pork ribs

2/3 cup ketchup

1 teaspoon orange zest

1/4 cup fresh lime juice

1 tablespoon Worcestershire sauce

1/4 cup brown sugar

1 teaspoon garlic powder

1 teaspoon shallot powder

1/2 teaspoon cumin powder 1/2 teaspoon mustard seeds

Directions

Firstly, place the ribs in a mixing dish.

Add the other ingredients and toss to coat evenly.

Next, transfer the ingredients to the air fryer grill pan; grill your ribs approximately 25 minutes at 390 degrees F. Serve warm and enjoy!

253. Herby Spaghetti with Mushroom

(Ready in about 25 minutes | Servings 4)

Ingredients

1 pound mushroom, chopped

1 carrot, finely chopped

1 stalk of celery, finely chopped

1 can tomatoes, chopped

1 small-sized onion, chopped

2 cloves garlic, finely minced

1/2 teaspoon seasoned salt

1/2 teaspoon ground black pepper

1/2 teaspoon dried oregano

1/2 teaspoon dried basil

1 box spaghetti

Directions

Place the mushrooms in an oven safe bowl; cook at 390 degrees F for 7 minutes.

Stir in the other ingredients, except for spaghetti, and cook for another 18 minutes. Serve over cooked spaghetti and enjoy!

254. Pork Chops with Caramel Applesauce

(Ready in about 25 minutes | Servings 4)

Ingredients

4 pork chops

2 garlic cloves, peeled and halved

1/4 teaspoon paprika

1/2 teaspoon salt

1/4 teaspoon ground black pepper

2 apples, peeled and sliced

2 tablespoons brown sugar

1/4 teaspoon freshly ground nutmeg

2 tablespoons olive oil

Directions

Rup pork chops with the garlic halves. Season pork chops with the paprika, salt and ground black pepper.

Cook for 13 minutes at 390 degrees F.

Meanwhile, in a sauté pan, simmer all remaining ingredients for about 8 minutes until apples are softened.

Pour the apple sauce over prepared pork chops and serve.

255. Cheesy Beef Egg Rolls

(Ready in about 20 minutes | Servings 4)

Ingredients

1 tablespoon canola oil

2 cloves garlic, minced

1 medium-sized onion, finely chopped

2 bell peppers, chopped

6 ounces roast beef, thinly sliced

1 teaspoon cayenne pepper

Salt and ground black pepper, to your liking

1/2 pound pepper jack cheese, shredded

8 egg roll skins

Directions

Heat the oil in a sauté pan. Sauté the garlic, onion, and peppers about 6 minutes, stirring continuously. Set aside.

In the same sauté pan, cook the beef until it is no longer pink. Season with cayenne pepper, salt, and black pepper; fold in the shredded cheese; stir to combine. Combine with the pepper mixture.

Place the meat/pepper mixture in center of each egg roll skin. Roll them, sealing the edges. Spritz each roll with a nonstick cooking spray.

Cook at 350 degrees F for 10 to 12 minutes. After that, increase the temperature to 400 degrees F and cook for 2 more minutes. Bon appétit!

256. Creamy Dijon Drumsticks

(Ready in about 25 minutes | Servings 4)

Ingredients

4 chicken drumsticks

1/2 cup milk

1 teaspoon Dijon mustard

1 tablespoon ginger, minced

1/2 teaspoon ground black pepper

1/4 teaspoon red pepper flakes, crushed

1/2 teaspoon sea salt

Directions

In a mixing bowl, combine all ingredients thoroughly.

Let it stand overnight in your refrigerator.

Cook the chicken at 375 degrees F for 25 minutes; flip the drumsticks over at half-time. Serve and enjoy!

257. Rustic Pork Ribs

(Ready in about 25 minutes | Servings 4)

Ingredients

1 rack of pork ribs

3 tablespoons dry red wine

1 tablespoon soy sauce

1/2 teaspoon dried thyme

1/2 teaspoon onion powder

1/2 teaspoon garlic powder

1/2 teaspoon ground black pepper

1 teaspoon smoke salt

1 tablespoon cornstarch

1/2 teaspoon olive oil

Directions

Begin by preheating your air fryer to 390 degrees F. Place all ingredients in a mixing bowl and let them marinate at least 1 hour.

After that, cook the marinated ribs approximately 25 minutes at 390 degrees F. Bon appétit!

258. Cauliflower Rice with Mushrooms

(Ready in about 35 minutes | Servings 4)

Ingredients

1 head cauliflower, broken into florets

2 tablespoons olive oil

4 tablespoons soy sauce

2 carrots, trimmed and chopped

3 cloves garlic, finely minced

1 teaspoon fresh ginger, grated

Salt and ground black pepper, to taste

1/2 teaspoon paprika

2 pounds canned mushrooms, sliced

Directions

In your food processor, pulse the cauliflower; you should have the size of rice.

Add the cauliflower rice to the air fryer. Next, add the remaining ingredients, except for canned mushrooms. Cook at 375 degrees F for 20 minutes.

Throw in the mushrooms and continue to cook for another 15 minutes. Enjoy!

259. Restaurant-Style Duck Loaf

(Ready in about 45 minutes | Servings 6)

Ingredients

2 pounds ground duck meat

1 cup evaporated milk

3 cups corn flakes, processed in a dry grains blender

2 eggs

3/4 teaspoon salt

1/2 teaspoon cayenne pepper

1/2 teaspoon ground black pepper

3/4 pound Swiss cheese, cubed

1/2 cup tomato ketchup

Directions

In a mixing dish, combine the ground meat, milk, corn flakes, and eggs; mix by hand. Add the salt, cayenne pepper, and black pepper.

Stir the cheese cubes into the mixture. Press the mixture into the loaf pan; top with tomato ketchup.

Place the pan into your air fryer and cook for 45 minutes at 390 degrees F. Bon appétit!

260. Ultimate Au Gratin Potatoes

(Ready in about 15 minutes | Servings 4)

Ingredients

4 medium potatoes, thinly sliced

1/4 cup vegetable broth

1/4 cup milk

1/4 cup soft cheese

Kosher salt and ground black pepper, to taste

1/4 cup Romano cheese, grated

Directions

In the mixing bowl, combine all ingredients, except Romano cheese. Transfer the mixture to the baking pan.

Sprinkle the Romano cheese evenly over the potatoes.

Bake at 330 degrees F for 15 minutes or until lightly browned. Bon appétit!

261. Mustard and Basil Shrimp

(Ready in about 35 minutes | Servings 4)

Ingredients

1 pound shrimp, shelled and deveined

2 cloves garlic, finely minced

Sea salt and freshly cracked black pepper, to your liking

1 tablespoon Dijon mustard

1 heaping tablespoon fresh basil, minced

1 tablespoon butter, melted

Directions

Start by mixing all of the above ingredients. Let it stand about 30 minutes.

Add the shrimp mixture to the air fryer basket; fry for about 5 minutes at 390 degrees F. Serve over mashed potatoes.

262. Cremini Mushroom and Chives Pizza

(Ready in about 20 minutes | Servings 4)

Ingredients

4 ounces prepared pizza dough

Nonstick cooking spray

1 cup cremini mushrooms, sliced

1 dried basil, crushed

1 teaspoon dried oregano, crushed

1 tablespoon olive oil

Sea salt and ground black pepper, to your liking

1 green bell pepper, chopped

1/2 cup chives, chopped

1/2 cup Cheddar cheese, shredded

Directions

Roll the pizza dough out. Add the dough to the tray; brush it with a nonstick cooking spray. Bake the dough at 350 degrees F for 5 minutes.

Turn the dough over, brush with the spray again, and bake an additional 5 minutes. Reserve.

Add the mushrooms, basil, oregano, olive oil, salt, black pepper, and bell pepper to an ovenproof dish. Air fry at 400 degrees F for 5 minutes until tender.

Spread the mushroom mixture over the reserved pizza crust, top with the chives and Cheddar cheese. Return to your air fryer and bake for 5 more minutes at 400 degrees F.

263. Lemon and Garlic Grilled Halibut

(Ready in about 45 minutes | Servings 4)

Ingredients

1 pound halibut steak

2 tablespoons butter, melted

2 cloves garlic, minced

2/3 cup soy sauce

1/2 cup chicken broth

1/4 cup sugar

1/4 cup of lemon juice

1/2 teaspoon sea salt

1/4 black pepper, preferably freshly ground

1 teaspoon cumin powder

Directions

Add all ingredients, except for halibut steak, to the sauté pan. Now, cook the mixture, bringing to a boil. Let it cool fully.

Put 1/2 of the marinade in a resalable bag. Place halibut steak in the marinade and let it stand about 30 minutes in the fridge.

Cook the halibut steaks for 10 to 12 minutes at 390 degrees F.

Serve halibut steak with the remaining marinade. Bon appétit!

264. Quick and Easy Cheese Ravioli

(Ready in about 20 minutes | Servings 4)

Ingredients

3 eggs, beaten

2 cups all-purpose flour

2 cups crumbled Ritz crackers

12 cheese ravioli, frozen

Directions

Take three shallow bowls. Place the eggs, flour, and crackers in separate bowls.

Then, dip your ravioli in the following way: egg, flour, egg, and crackers.

Cook in the air fryer basket at 370 degrees F for about 18 minutes, turning over halfway. Work with batches. Serve with the sauce of choice.

265. Italian Sausage with Roasted Vegetables

(Ready in about 35 minutes | Servings 4)

Ingredients

2 red onions, sliced

4 bell peppers, sliced

1 Serrano pepper, cut lengthwise

2 sprigs thyme

1 teaspoon dried oregano

1 tablespoon olive oil

1 pound Italian sausage

Directions

Arrange the onions and peppers on the bottom of the air fryer basket. Sprinkle thyme and oregano over them. Drizzle with olive oil.

Then, place the sausage on top of the vegetables.

Roast for about 35 minutes at 370 degrees F or until the sausages are lightly browned; make sure to stir once halfway through. Bon appétit!

266. Pepper Steak Rolls

(Ready in about 20 minutes | Servings 6)

Ingredients

1 tablespoon olive oil

1 red bell pepper, seeded and chopped

1 orange bell pepper, seeded and chopped

1 green bell pepper, seeded and chopped

1 medium-sized onion, finely chopped

1 (6-ounce) package sliced steak, frozen

Salt and ground black pepper, to your liking

1/2 pound Colby cheese, shredded

12 roll wrappers

Directions

Heat olive oil in a sauté pan. Sauté the peppers and onion until they're softened, about 6 minutes. Set aside.

In the same sauté pan, cook the steak until cooked through. Chop the meat and set it aside. Add the salt, black pepper and shredded cheese; stir to combine.

Then, lay the roll wrappers on a clean surface. Divide the meat mixture among the wrappers. Top with the pepper mixture. Lastly, roll them up and spritz with the canola oil spray.

Cook at 350 degrees F for 10 to 12 minutes. After that, increase the temperature to 400 degrees F and cook for 2 more minutes. Enjoy!

267. Old-Fashioned Beef Chili

(Ready in about 45 minutes | Servings 6)

Ingredients

1 tablespoon melted lard

1 yellow onion, finely chopped

2 hot chili peppers, seeded and finely minced

1 pound ground beef

1 ½ cups roasted vegetable stock

1 teaspoon coriander

1 can tomatoes, diced

1 can black beans, drained and rinsed

1 teaspoon kosher salt

1/4 teaspoon ground black pepper, or to taste

Directions

Place the lard, onion, and chili peppers in the air fryer baking dish. Cook for 5 minutes at 350 degrees F.

Add the beef and cook for 6 minutes longer. Now, pause the machine and add the stock, coriander, and diced tomatoes. Cook for 20 minutes longer, stirring once.

Throw in the beans; season with salt and black pepper; continue cooking another 10 minutes or until beans are heated through. Taste, adjust the seasonings and serve.

268. Mexican-Style Turkey Breasts

(Ready in about 25 minutes | Servings 4)

Ingredients

1/4 cup Parmesan cheese, shredded

1 cup tortilla chips, crumbled

1/2 teaspoon sea salt

1/2 teaspoon ground black pepper, or to taste

1/2 tablespoon chili powder

2 tablespoons cream cheese

1/2 cup mayonnaise

1 turkey breast, quartered

Directions

In a mixing dish, thoroughly combine Parmesan, crumbled tortilla chips, salt, black pepper, and chili powder.

In another mixing dish, combine cream cheese and mayonnaise. Coat the turkey breasts with the cheese/mayo mixture.

Dredge chicken breasts in the breadcrumb mixture. Then, cook for about 25 minutes at 350 degrees F. Bon appétit!

269. Avocado and Cheese Roll-Ups

(Ready in about 15 minutes | Servings 6)

Ingredients

2 avocados, cut into small chunks

1/4 cup soft cheese

1/2 teaspoon garlic salt

1/2 teaspoon red pepper flakes, crushed

24 egg roll wrappers

For the Sauce:

1 avocado

2 tablespoons yogurt

1/4 cup buttermilk

1 tablespoon fresh lemon juice

1 tablespoon fresh cilantro, chopped

1/4 cup green onions, finely chopped

2 cloves garlic, finely minced

Directions

In a mixing dish, stir together the avocado, soft cheese, salt, and red pepper.

Divide the mixture among wraps and roll them up. Seal the edges using the water. Lightly brush each roll with a nonstick cooking spray.

Bake for about 12 minutes at 400 degrees F in a single layer, working in batches.

To make the sauce, pulse all ingredients in your food processor until smooth.

270. Greek-Style Parmesan Potatoes

(Ready in about 30 minutes | Servings 4)

Ingredients

3/4 teaspoon paprika

Sea salt and ground black pepper, to your liking

1 teaspoon dried basil

1/2 teaspoon dried oregano

1/2 teaspoon dried rosemary

4 garlic cloves, chopped

2 olive oil

1 tablespoon balsamic vinegar

1 ½ cups roasted vegetable broth

3 baking potatoes, peeled and cut into wedges

1 cup Parmesan cheese, grated

Directions

In a large bowl, toss all ingredients, except Parmesan, until the potatoes are completely coated.

Transfer the mixture to a baking dish. Then, transfer the dish to the air fryer. Cover with foil and air-fry for 20 minutes at 400 degrees F.

Scatter Parmesan cheese over the potatoes. Bake for another 8 minutes at 370 degrees F. Eat warm.

271. Mango Salmon Steaks

(Ready in about 2 hours 10 minutes | Servings 2)

Ingredients

2 salmon fillets

2 tablespoons olive oil

1 teaspoon cayenne pepper

Ground black pepper and salt, to your liking

1/4 teaspoon garlic powder

1/2 teaspoon shallot powder

1 tablespoon lemon juice

1/3 cup dry white wine

1 teaspoon dried rosemary, crushed

1 mango, peeled, seeded, and diced

Directions

Wash and pat the salmon dry using the paper towels. Drizzle them with olive oil.

Season the salmon with cayenne pepper, black pepper, salt, garlic powder, and shallot powder. In a separate bowl, prepare the marinade by mixing together the lemon juice, white wine, and rosemary.

Place the salmon in the marinade. Cover and refrigerate for at least 2 hours.

Arrange the salmon steaks on an air fryer grill basket. Bake at 330 degrees F for 8 minutes. Garnish with the diced mango and serve.

272. Easy Chinese Dumplings

(Ready in about 10 minutes | Servings 6)

Ingredients

24 wonton wrappers

For the Filling:

1 teaspoon chili-garlic sauce

2 tablespoons Chinese chives, chopped

1 pound mixed ground meat, cooked and crumbled

1 tablespoon dry white wine

1 teaspoon olive oil

Directions

In a large bowl, combine filling ingredients; mix until thoroughly combined. Then, divide the filling among the wrappers.

Then, fold each dumpling in half and pinch to seal. Transfer the dumplings to the air fryer.

Brush them lightly with a cooking spray; bake at 400 degrees F for 10 minutes, turning over halfway through. Serve.

273. Wonton Taco Cups

(Ready in about 10 minutes | Servings 8)

Ingredients

1/2 pound ground pork, browned and drained

1/2 pound ground beef, browned and drained

1 envelope taco seasoning

1 (10-ounce) can tomatoes with chilies, diced and drained

1 bell pepper, seeded and chopped

32 wonton wrappers

1 cup Cheddar cheese, shredded

Directions

Combine the pork, beef, taco seasoning, diced tomatoes, and bell pepper; mix well.

Line all the muffin cups with wonton wrappers. Spritz with a nonstick cooking oil. Divide the beef filling among wrappers; top with the shredded cheese.

Bake at 370 degrees F for about 10 minutes or until heated through.

274. Grilled Cheese Sandwiches

(Ready in about 10 minutes | Servings 2)

Ingredients

1 tablespoon softened butter

4 slices bread, per sandwich

2 slices cheese

Directions

Butter two slices of bread. Place one slice on the rack. Add the cheese slice; top with the second slice of buttered bread.

Bake in an air fryer grill basket at 400 degrees F for 8 minutes, turning halfway through. Eat warm.

275. Spicy Vegetarian Burgers

(Ready in about 20 minutes | Servings 4)

Ingredients

16 ounces canned beans

2 cloves garlic, minced

1/2 cup scallions, finely chopped

1 teaspoon cumin powder

1 small bunch coriander, chopped

1 tablespoon fresh salsa

1 egg, well-beaten

1 teaspoon cayenne pepper

Sea salt and ground black pepper, to taste

2 tablespoons salsa

1/2 cup crushed corn flakes cereal

4 whole meal burger buns

Directions

Firstly, in a mixing bowl, mash the beans with a potato masher.

Add the remaining ingredient, except for the buns. Wet your hands and shape the mixture into 4 patties.

Bake your burgers in the air fryer grill pan at 390 degrees F for 15 to 18 minutes.

To serve: Split the buns in half and add the bean burgers. Top with some extra salsa and onions, if desired. Enjoy!

276. Holiday Chicken Cups

(Ready in about 10 minutes | Servings 6)

Ingredients

2 tablespoons mild wing sauce

1/4 cup soft cheese

1 cup chicken breasts, cooked and diced

2 ounces blue cheese, crumbled

1 teaspoon dried rosemary, crushed

12 wonton wrappers

Directions

In a bowl, combine together the wing sauce and soft cheese. Add the chicken breasts, blue cheese, and dried rosemary. Stir until they're just combined.

Then, place 1 wonton wrapper in each mini-muffin cup; press down to create a cup. Fill each cup with the chicken mixture.

Bake at 330 degrees F for 10 minutes, or until the cheese is bubbling. Enjoy!

277. Herbed Steak Dinner for Two

(Ready in about 45 minutes | Servings 2)

Ingredients

2 sprigs thyme, finely chopped

2 sprigs rosemary, finely chopped

1 bunch cilantro, finely chopped

4 cloves garlic, finely chopped

2 tablespoons canola oil

2 steaks

1/2 teaspoon sea salt

1/2 teaspoon ground black pepper, to taste

1 teaspoon cayenne pepper

Directions

In a small-sized mixing bowl, combine the thyme, rosemary, cilantro, garlic, and canola oil.

Rub each steak with the spice mix; sprinkle them with salt, black pepper, and cayenne pepper. Let them sit for 30 minutes.

Transfer your steaks to the air fryer pan. Roast at 400 degrees F for about 15 minutes, turning it halfway through the cooking time.

278. Turkey Stuffed Potatoes

(Ready in about 20 minutes | Servings 4)

Ingredients

For the Sauce:

1 tablespoon butter

1 tablespoon flour

Sea salt and ground black pepper, to your liking

1/2 cup milk

10 slices yellow cheese

For the Filling:

1/2 pound ground turkey

1 small-sized onion, finely chopped

2 cloves garlic, minced

Sea salt and red pepper flakes, to your liking

1 teaspoon soy sauce

4 tablespoons tomato puree

4 potatoes, baked

Directions

In a saucepan, melt the butter over medium flame. Then, add the flour and stir constantly for about 1 minute. Now, add the salt, black pepper, and milk.

Bring it to a simmer, stirring frequently. When the sauce has thickened, remove from the heat; now, fold in the cheese and stir until it is completely melted.

To prepare the filling, cook the ground turkey along with the onion and garlic. Drain off the extra fat; stir in the salt, red pepper, soy sauce, and tomato puree; now, fold in the cheese sauce.

Scoop out the flesh from each potato, creating a shell. Chop 1/2 of the potato flesh; add the potato flesh to the turkey mixture.

Next, fill the potato shells with the mixture. Bake at 330 degrees F for 18 minutes.

279. Crab Cake Burgers

(Ready in about 10 minutes | Servings 4)

Ingredients

1/2 pound jumbo lump crab meat

10 saltine crackers, finely crushed

2 tablespoons mayonnaise

1 teaspoon Dijon mustard

1 teaspoon soy sauce

1 egg, beaten

1/2 teaspoon salt

1 tablespoon butter

Directions

Combine all ingredients in a mixing bowl. Form the mixture into four patties.

Bush them with a nonstick cooking spray. Arrange the patties on the bottom of a baking pan; then, transfer the pan to the air fryer.

Bake at 370 degrees F for 10 minutes, turning halfway through. Serve on burger buns.

280. Asian-Style Beef Dumplings

(Ready in about 10 minutes | Servings 6)

Ingredients

1 teaspoon chili sauce

1 tablespoon sesame seeds

1 tablespoon seasoned rice vinegar

1 tablespoon sesame oil

1/3 cup soy sauce

30 wonton wrappers

For the Filling:

1 small-sized onions, chopped

2 garlic cloves, minced

1 pound ground beef, cooked and crumbled

Directions

In a small-sized mixing bowl, combine chili sauce, sesame seeds, seasoned rice vinegar, sesame and soy sauce; mix until thoroughly combined.

After that, combine all ingredients for the filling. Place the wrappers on a clean and dry surface. Now, divide the filling among the wrappers.

Then, fold each dumpling in half and pinch to seal. Transfer the dumplings to your air fryer.

Brush them lightly with a nonstick cooking spray. Bake at 400 degrees F for 10 minutes, turning over halfway through. Serve.

281. Dinner Turkey Nachos

(Ready in about 10 minutes | Servings 4)

Ingredients

1 teaspoon garlic powder

1 teaspoon shallot powder

1 teaspoon ground cumin

1/4 teaspoon ground black pepper

1 teaspoon salt

2 cups turkey breasts, shredded

Tortilla chips

2 tomatoes, diced

9 ounces canned beans, rinsed and drained

1 cup yellow cheese, shredded

1 jalapeño pepper, finely chopped

Directions

Stir together the garlic powder, shallot powder, ground cumin, black pepper, and salt in a bowl. Throw in the turkey breasts and toss to coat.

Add a layer of foil to the air fryer basket. Arrange the tortilla chips on the bottom of the basket. Add the turkey, followed by the tomatoes and canned beans.

Top with the yellow cheese and chopped jalapeño. Bake approximately 10 minutes at 300 degrees F. Enjoy!

282. Yummy Chorizo and Veggie Dinner

(Ready in about 35 minutes | Servings 6)

Ingredients

1 pound white mushrooms, cut into large chunks

1 shallot, cut into wedges

1 bell pepper, seeded and sliced

1 Serrano pepper, seeded and sliced

2 sprigs thyme

1 bay leaf

1 teaspoon mustard seeds

1 teaspoon fennel seeds

1 tablespoon melted lard

1 pound Chorizo sausages

Directions

Place all vegetables and seasonings on the bottom of the air fryer basket. Add the melted lard and stir to coat well.

Top with the sausage.

Roast at 370 degrees F for 30 to 35 minutes or until the sausages are lightly browned, turning all ingredients halfway through. Serve warm with crusty bread, if desired. Enjoy!

283. Juicy Pork Ribs Ole

(Ready in about 1 hour 25 minutes | Servings 4)

Ingredients

1 rack of pork ribs

1/2 cup low-fat milk

1 tablespoon envelope taco seasoning mix

1 can tomato sauce

1/2 teaspoon ground black pepper

1 teaspoon seasoned salt

1 tablespoon cornstarch

1 teaspoon canola oil

Directions

Place all ingredients in a mixing dish; let them marinate for 1 hour.

Then, cook the marinated ribs approximately 25 minutes at 390 degrees F. Work with batches. Bon appétit!

284. Crunchy Catfish Fillets

(Ready in about 10 minutes | Servings 4)

Ingredients

1/2 pound catfish fillets

1 tablespoon olive oil

1/2 teaspoon salt

1/2 cup corn flakes, crushed

1 teaspoon Old Bay seasoning

1 teaspoon dried dill weed

1/4 cup four

1 egg, beaten

Directions

Drizzle fish fillets with olive oil. Season them with salt. In a shallow dish, combine corn flakes with Old Bay seasoning and dill.

Dip each fish fillet in the flour. Then, dip each fillet in the beaten egg mixture.

Afterward, coat them with the corn flakes mixture. Shake off excess breading.

Transfer coated fish to the food basket and cook for about 8 to 10 minutes at 390 degrees F. Bon appétit!

285. Sugar-Lime Glazed Halibut

(Ready in about 45 minutes | Servings 4)

Ingredients

1/2 cup of mirin

2/3 cup soy sauce

1/4 cup lime juice

2 tablespoons sugar

1 tablespoon cilantro, chopped

1/2 teaspoon ground ginger

1 pound halibut steak

Salt and ground black pepper, to taste

Directions

Combine the mirin, soy sauce, lime juice, sugar, cilantro, and ginger in a pan; bring it to a boil and cook until reduced by half. Let it cool.

Add 1/2 of the marinade to a bowl. Place the halibut in the marinade; allow it to stand for about 30 minutes in the refrigerator.

Place the halibut steaks in the food basket. Season the steaks with salt and black pepper. Cook for 12 minutes at 390 degrees F. Brush with the remaining marinade and serve. Bon appétit!

286. Chipotle Pork Ribs

(Ready in about 25 minutes | Servings 4)

Ingredients

4 portions pork ribs

1/2 cup milk

1 tablespoon fresh chipotle pepper, finely minced

1 teaspoon Dijon mustard

1/2 teaspoon sea salt

1/2 teaspoon ground black pepper

1/4 teaspoon red pepper flakes, crushed

Directions

In a mixing bowl, combine all of the above items. Let them marinate overnight in the refrigerator.

Cook pork ribs at 375 degrees F for 25 minutes, working in batches; flip them over at half-time. Serve warm over the mashed potatoes.

287. Curried Prawns with Dill Sauce

(Ready in about 40 minutes | Servings 4)

Ingredients

8 prawns

1/2 cup coconut milk

1 teaspoon red chili powder

1 teaspoon turmeric powder

1 teaspoon cumin powder

1 teaspoon salt

1/4 teaspoon ground black pepper

3 egg whites

2 tablespoons flour

1/2 cup Greek yogurt

1 heaping tablespoon fresh chopped dill

Directions

Add the prawns and coconut milk to the mixing dish; then, stir in red chili powder, turmeric powder, and cumin powder; let it marinate for about 30 minutes.

Season the prawns with salt and black pepper.

Beat egg whites until foamy; add the flour and mix to combine well. Dip each prawn in this batter.

Fry the prawns at 350 degrees F for about 8 minutes.

Meanwhile, make the sauce by mixing Greek yogurt and dill. Serve fried prawns with the dill sauce and enjoy!

288. Chorizo and Leek Meatballs

(Ready in about 15 minutes | Servings 4)

Ingredients

1/2 pound chorizo

1 medium-sized leek, finely chopped

2 garlic cloves, minced

1 teaspoon dried dill weed

1/4 cup breadcrumbs

Salt and ground black pepper, to your liking

Directions

Mix well all ingredients.

Form the mixture into the balls. Transfer the meatballs to your air fryer.

Fry the meatballs at 350 degrees F for 15 minutes.

289. Easy Homemade Croutons

(Ready in about 10 minutes | Servings 6)

Ingredients

10 slices whole meal bread

2 teaspoons garlic salt

2 tablespoons butter

Directions

Chop the bread into the chunks and place them in the air fryer basket.

Toss bread chunks with garlic salt and butter; now, cook the chunks for 8 minutes at 390 degrees F. Serve with your favorite salad.

290. Grandma's Old-Fashioned Fish Cakes

(Ready in about 15 minutes | Servings 6)

Ingredients

1 cup mashed potatoes

2 cups catfish

1 cup scallions

2 cloves garlic

1 tablespoon olive oil

1 teaspoon grated lemon rind

1 tablespoon Worcester sauce

1 teaspoon sea salt

1/4 teaspoon ground black pepper

1/2 teaspoon cayenne pepper

1 teaspoon dried rosemary, crushed

1/4 cup breadcrumbs

Directions

Combine all ingredients in a mixing dish. Shape the mixture into fishcakes; place them in the refrigerator for 3 hours.

Cook in the air fryer for 15 minutes at 390 degrees F.

291. Dinner Party Thai Meatballs

(Ready in about 15 minutes | Servings 4)

Ingredients

1 pound ground beef

1 teaspoon garlic puree

1 onion, finely chopped

1 tablespoon soy sauce

1 tablespoon red Thai curry paste

1 teaspoon Five-spice blend

Salt and ground black pepper, to your liking

Directions

Mix all the ingredients in a bowl.

Shape the mixture into balls.

Cook the meatballs for 15 minutes at 350 degrees F.

292. Pork Chops with Apple Sauce

(Ready in about 25 minutes | Servings 4)

Ingredients

4 pork chops

1/2 teaspoon sea salt

1/2 teaspoon ground black pepper

2 apples, peeled and sliced

2 tablespoons brown sugar

1/4 teaspoon allspice

2 tablespoons butter

Directions

Season pork chops with salt and ground black pepper. Cook in your air fryer for 13 minutes at 390 degrees F.

In a sauté pan, simmer the apples, sugar, allspice, and butter. Cook for about 8 minutes until the apples are softened. Pour the sauce over the pork chops and serve warm.

DESSERTS

293. Lemon Blackberry Coffee Cake

(Ready in about 15 minutes | Servings 8)

Ingredients

For the Cake:

1/2 cup old-fashioned rolled oats

1 cup flour

1/4 cup sugar

1 teaspoon baking powder

1 teaspoon baking soda

1 teaspoon grated ginger

1/4 teaspoon grated nutmeg

2 tablespoons butter

1/2 cup milk

2 large egg whites, lightly beaten

1/2 cup blackberries

For the Glaze:

1/4 cup powdered sugar

1 teaspoon lemon juice

1 teaspoon vanilla paste

1 teaspoon lemon peel, finely grated

Directions

Lightly grease two mini loaf pans. Grind rolled oats in a food processor.

Add the oats, flour, sugar, baking powder, baking soda, ginger, and nutmeg to a large bowl. Add the butter and mix until mixture resembles coarse crumbs.

Stir in the milk and egg whites; fold in blackberries. Scrape the mixture into the prepared pans. Bake at 300 degrees F for 15 minutes.

To make the glaze, combine the powdered sugar with lemon juice and vanilla paste. Spread the glaze over coffee cake. For decoration: sprinkle with lemon peel.

294. Apple and Walnut Roll-Ups

(Ready in about 10 minutes | Servings 8)

Ingredients

16 egg roll wrappers

1 (12-ounce) can apple pie filling

1/2 cup walnuts, chopped

1/2 cup powdered sugar

1/2 teaspoon vanilla essence

1/2 teaspoon ground cinnamon

1/4 teaspoon ground cloves

4 tablespoons melted ghee

Directions

Lay roll wraps on a clean work surface.

Divide the pie filling and walnuts among the wrappers. Now, fold up the wrappers like burritos. Lightly brush with the oil; transfer them to the air fryer basket.

Bake at 350 degrees F for about 10 minutes; work with batches. Meanwhile, combine the sugar, vanilla, cinnamon, and cloves.

Next, brush the roll-ups with melted ghee. Dust the sugar mixture over the top of the roll-ups. Enjoy!

295. Berry Cheesecake Rolls

(Ready in about 10 minutes | Servings 8)

Ingredients

Cake pan spray

8 ounces cream cheese, softened

1/2 cup powdered sugar

1 teaspoon pure vanilla extract

16 egg roll wrappers

4 cups blueberries, chopped

1/4 cup butterscotch chips

Directions

Lightly grease a baking sheet with a cake pan spray; set it aside.

Whip together the cream cheese, sugar, and vanilla. Divide the mixture among egg roll wrappers; now, add a small scoop of blueberries.

Then, roll the wrappers and seal the edges. Transfer the rolls to the prepared baking sheet. Bake in batches for about 10 minutes at 375 degrees F. Make sure to turn over halfway through.

Meanwhile, microwave butterscotch chips, uncovered, about 1 minute or until they have completely softened. Drizzle cheesecake rolls with melted butterscotch chips. Bon appétit!

296. Chocolate Cheesecake Cups

(Ready in about 20 minutes | Servings 8)

Ingredients

For the Crust:

1 cup graham cracker crumbs

2 tablespoons sugar

1 teaspoon pure vanilla extract

A pinch of salt

2 tablespoons butter, melted

For the Cheesecake:

1 (8-ounce) package cream cheese, softened

1/3 cup sugar

1 medium-sized egg

1/2 teaspoon ground anise star

1 cup chocolate chips

Directions

Firstly, coat eight cups of a mini muffin pan with paper liners.

Now, prepare the batter by mixing all ingredients for the crust. Evenly divide the batter among muffin cups.

To make the cheesecake, in a mixing bowl, beat together the cheese and sugar until uniform and smooth. Fold in the egg and ground anise; beat again until everything is well combined.

Add approximately 1 tablespoon of chocolate chips to each of the muffin cups. Divide cheesecake batter between the cups. Top with another layer of chocolate chips.

Bake for about 20 minutes at 330 degrees F, or until it is set. Store in the refrigerator.

297. Nana's Famous Brownies

(Ready in about 10 minutes | Servings 4)

Ingredients

3/4 cup chocolate-hazelnut spread of choice

1 egg

1/4 cup self-rising flour

Directions

In a bowl, mix all of the above ingredients together. Then, lightly spray a 6-inch metal square pan with a cake pan spray. The pan should fit in your air fryer.

Scrape the mixture into the pan; distribute the batter evenly with a spatula.

Next, bake for about 10 minutes at 330 degrees F.

298. Banana-Chocolate Wontons

(Ready in about 10 minutes | Servings 8)

Ingredients

16 wonton wrappers

1 egg, lightly beaten

1 cup chocolate-hazelnut spread

1 banana, thinly sliced

1/2 cup granulated sugar

Directions

Coat the edges of each wrapper with the beaten egg. Divide the chocolate-hazelnut spread among wonton wrappers.

Then, add banana slices and fold the wrappers diagonally in half over the filling; press and seal the edges.

Add the sugar to a shallow bowl. Spray the wontons with a nonstick cooking oil; dip each side in the sugar.

Working in batches, place a single layer of wontons in the air fryer basket. Then, bake at 370 degrees F for 8 minutes, turning over halfway through. Serve at room temperature.

299. Mini Strawberry Pies

(Ready in about 10 minutes | Servings 8)

Ingredients

1/2 cup powdered sugar

1/4 teaspoon ground cloves

1/2 teaspoon ground cinnamon

1/2 teaspoon ground anise star

1 large-sized can flaky-style biscuit dough

1 (12-ounce) can strawberry pie filling

Directions

In a shallow dish, combine the sugar, ground cloves, cinnamon, and anise star.

Roll each section of the biscuit dough into a round circle. Divide the strawberry pie filling among the circles.

Dip each roll in the sugar mixture; roll to coat well. Spray them with canola oil.

Transfer them to the air fryer basket and bake at 330 degrees F for about 10 minutes; work with batches and allow them to cool completely before serving time.

300. Famous Chocolate Alaskas

(Ready in about 10 minutes | Servings 6)

Ingredients

4 egg whites

A pinch of salt

1/2 teaspoon cream of tartar

1/2 teaspoon vanilla paste

1/4 teaspoon pure orange extract

1/4 teaspoon ground anise star

1/4 cup powdered sugar

6 pre-made dessert shells

1 pound chocolate ice cream

Directions

To make the meringue, beat egg whites until foamy; now, stir in the salt, cream of tartar, vanilla, orange extract, and anise star; throw in the sugar and continue to beat until shiny peaks form.

Fill the center of each shell with ice cream. Top with a layer of meringue. Bake in your air fryer at 420 degrees F for 4 minutes. Enjoy!

301. The Best Peach Cobbler Ever

(Ready in about 20 minutes | Servings 6)

Ingredients

1 pound peaches, pitted and cut into wedges

1/2 cup flour

1/2 cup sugar

1 teaspoon vanilla paste

1/2 teaspoon ground cinnamon

1/4 teaspoon freshly grated ginger

1 tablespoon cold butter

Directions

Arrange the peaches on the bottom of a baking dish.

In a mixing dish, combine the remaining ingredients; sprinkle this topping over the peaches.

Bake at 330 degrees F for about 20 minutes or until golden. Serve at room temperature and enjoy!

302. Cinnamon Fried Bananas

(Ready in about 10 minutes | Servings 2)

Ingredients

1/2 cup flour

A pinch of salt

A pinch of freshly grated nutmeg

2 eggs, well-whisked

3/4 cup bread crumbs

1 teaspoon ground cinnamon

1 tablespoon turbinado sugar

2 medium-sized bananas, quartered

1 tablespoon melted coconut oil

Directions

Combine the flour, salt, and nutmeg in one bowl. In another bowl, place the eggs; add the bread crumbs to the third bowl.

Dust the bananas with the cinnamon and sugar. Dip the banana pieces in the flour, then in the egg; lastly, dredge them in the breadcrumbs. Drizzle melted coconut butter over prepared bananas.

Transfer the banana pieces to the air fryer basket. Bake at 350 degrees F for 8 minutes, turning once during the cooking time. Transfer them to a serving platter and serve at room temperature.

303. Quick and Easy Lava Cake

(Ready in about 15 minutes | Servings 4)

Ingredients

Cocoa powder, for dusting

1/3 cup butter

1/2 cup chopped chocolate

1/4 cup sugar

2 tablespoons all-purpose flour

2 eggs

Directions

Grease the bottom and sides of four ramekins using a nonstick cooking spray. Them, dust each ramekin with the cocoa powder.

Next, microwave the butter and chopped chocolate until it is melted and smooth. Add the sugar and flour to the butter/chocolate mixture. Fold in the eggs; mix well until smooth.

Pour the batter into the ramekins. Transfer the ramekins to the air fryer. Bake at 330 degrees F for about 15 minutes, or until the edges are set. Serve warm.

304. Everyday Banana Dessert

(Ready in about 40 minutes | Servings 4)

Ingredients

4 bananas, sliced lengthwise

1 cup sugar

A pinch of salt

A pinch of ground cloves

1/2 teaspoon pure vanilla extract

2 tablespoons cold butter

Directions

Grease a baking dish; place the banana slices on the bottom of the baking dish.

In a mixing dish, combine the sugar, salt, cloves and vanilla. The, sprinkle the sugar mixture over the banana layer.

Cut cold butter into crumbs and scatter them over the layers. Air-fryer for 40 minutes at 375 degrees F. Serve immediately or store in the refrigerator until serving time.

305. Baked Apples with Blackberry Jam

(Ready in about 30 minutes | Servings 4)

Ingredients

4 Fuji apples, cut into halves

1 tablespoon fresh lemon juice

1/2 teaspoon ground cinnamon

4 tablespoons blackberry jam

2 tablespoons flour

3 tablespoons butter, cold and diced

3 tablespoons sugar

1/2 cup oats

Directions

Take an apple and create a hole with a melon baller; repeat with the remaining apples. Drizzle the inside with fresh lemon juice.

Dust with the ground cinnamon. Add 1 tablespoon of jam to each hole.

Then, make the topping by mixing together the remaining ingredients.

Transfer the apples to a baking dish. Bake at 330 degrees F about 30 minutes or until the apples are tender.

306. Coconut and Chocolate Wontons

(Ready in about 10 minutes | Servings 8)

Ingredients

2 eggs, lightly beaten

1/4 teaspoon ground anise star

20 wonton wrappers

1 ¼ cups chocolate spread

1/4 cup coconut flakes, thinly sliced

Melted butter, for brushing

1/2 cup white sugar

Directions

Beat the eggs with ground anise star until well combined. Brush the edges of each wrapper with the egg mixture. Divide the chocolate spread among the wrappers.

Now, add the coconut flakes and fold the wrappers diagonally in half over the filling; press and seal the edges.

Throw the sugar into a shallow plate. Brush the wontons with melted butter; dip the wontons in the sugar.

Bake at 370 degrees F for 8 minutes, turning over halfway through; work with batches. Dust with some extra coconut flakes, if desired. Bon appétit!

307. Easy Brownies with Walnuts

(Ready in about 10 minutes | Servings 4)

Ingredients

3/4 cup chocolate spread

1/2 cup walnuts, finely chopped

1 egg

1 tablespoon honey

1/4 cup all-purpose flour

1 teaspoon baking powder

Directions

In a mixing dish, thoroughly combine all of the above ingredients together. Then, coat a baking pan with a cooking spray.

Spoon mixture into the baking pan. Bake your brownie for about 10 minutes at 330 degrees F.

308. Cranberry and Apple Dumplings

(Ready in about 25 minutes | Servings 2)

Ingredients

1 tablespoon granulated sugar

1/4 teaspoon ground cinnamon

2 tablespoons dried cranberries

2 sheets puff pastry

2 cooking apples, peeled and cored

2 tablespoons butter, melted

Directions

In a mixing dish, thoroughly combine the sugar, cinnamon, and cranberries.

Place an apple on one puff pastry sheet. Now, stuff your apples with the sugar/cranberry mixture.

Fold the pastry around the apple. Brush it with the melted butter. Then, cook your dumplings about 25 minutes at 350 degrees F. Serve at room temperature.

309. Double-Berry Pancakes

(Ready in about 10 minutes | Servings 6)

Ingredients

1 cup blackberries or raspberries

1 cup strawberries, hulled and quartered

2 tablespoons sugar

1 tablespoon lime juice

Pancakes, to serve

Maple syrup, to serve

Directions

Add the rinsed berries to the air fryer pan.

In a mixing bowl, combine the sugar with the lime juice until it is completely dissolved. Now, drizzle the sugar mixture over the top of your berries.

Cook for 8 minutes at 350 degrees F. Meanwhile, prepare the pancakes according to your favorite recipe.

Serve the berry topping with pancakes. Top with maple syrup and serve warm.

310. Quick and Easy Mocha Brownies

(Ready in about 10 minutes | Servings 6)

Ingredients

1 tablespoon instant coffee granules

2 eggs, well whisked

1 cup all-purpose flour

1 teaspoon baking powder

1/2 teaspoon baking soda

1 cup chocolate spread

Directions

In a mixing dish, thoroughly combine all of the above ingredients together. Treat a baking pan with a cooking spray.

Spoon mixture into the baking pan. Bake your brownie for about 10 minutes at 330 degrees F.

Transfer it to a cooling rack. Allow it to cool slightly before slicing and serving.

311. Apple and Pear Cobbler

(Ready in about 20 minutes | Servings 6)

Ingredients

1/2 pound cooking apples, cored and cut into wedges

1/2 pound cooking pears, cored and cut into wedges

1 tablespoon lemon juice

1/2 teaspoon ground cinnamon

1/2 cup sugar

1/2 cup flour

1/4 teaspoon freshly grated nutmeg

1 tablespoon butter

Directions

Arrange the apples and pears on the bottom of a baking dish. Drizzle lemon juice over them; sprinkle with ground cinnamon.

In a mixing bowl, combine the other items; sprinkle this topping over the fruit.

Bake at 330 degrees F for about 20 minutes or until golden. Serve and enjoy!

312. Tangy Pineapple Fritters

(Ready in about 10 minutes | Servings 4)

Ingredients

1/2 cup flour

2 eggs, well whisked

3/4 cup breadcrumbs

8 pieces fresh pineapple rings

1 tablespoon melted butter

1 tablespoon fresh lime juice

Directions

Place the flour on a plate. In another plate or shallow bowl, place the eggs; add the breadcrumbs to the third plate.

Dip the pineapple rings in the flour, then in the egg; lastly, dredge them in the breadcrumbs. Drizzle melted butter over them.

Transfer the banana pieces to the air fryer basket. Bake at 350 degrees F for 4 minutes; pause the machine and drizzle fresh lime juice over them. To serve: place two pineapple rings on a serving plate and top with a scoop of ice cream.

313. Chocolate Roll Crescents

(Ready in about 10 minutes | Servings 4)

Ingredients

1 can refrigerated crescent dinner rolls (4 squares)

1/4 cup chocolate spread

1 egg, lightly whisked

1/2 cup confectioner's sugar

3 tablespoons heavy cream

Directions

Unroll crescent dough on a dry and clean surface and separate squares.

Place 2 tablespoons of the chocolate spread in the center of each square; fold the dough over to make a triangle. Brush each triangle with the whisked egg.

Bake at 350 degrees F for 10 minutes, working with batches.

To make the frosting: In a small-sized mixing dish, beat the confectioner's sugar with heavy cream until thoroughly combined. Drizzle the tops of your rolls with frosting (for example, you can use a zig-zag look).

314. Bourbon Berry Cobbler

(Ready in about 20 minutes | Servings 6)

Ingredients

1/2 pound fresh blackberries

1/2 pound fresh blueberries

2 tablespoons bourbon

1/4 teaspoon ground cloves

1/2 teaspoon ground cinnamon

1/2 cup sugar

1/2 cup flour

1 tablespoon butter

Directions

Place the berries on the bottom of a baking dish. Drizzle them with the bourbon.

In a mixing bowl, combine the other ingredients; sprinkle the topping over the berries.

Bake at 330 degrees F for about 20 minutes. Enjoy!

315. The Easiest Lemon Cake Ever

(Ready in about 15 minutes | Servings 8)

Ingredients

For the Cake:

1 cup sugar

1 cup flour

2 sticks butter, at room temperature

3 eggs

1 teaspoon baking powder

1 tablespoon lemon zest

For the Glaze:

1/4 cup confectioners' sugar

2 tablespoons milk

1/2 teaspoon pure vanilla essence

2 tablespoons lemon juice

Directions

Treat two baking pans with a nonstick cooking spray.

Add all the cake ingredients to a bowl; mix using a hand mixer until creamy. Divide the batter among pans. Bake at 350 degrees F for 15 minutes or until golden.

Meanwhile, prepare the glaze by mixing all the items. Next, drizzle each cake with the prepared glaze.

316. Cinnamon Roll Bread Pudding with Almonds

(Ready in about 40 minutes | Servings 6)

Ingredients

6 unfrosted cinnamon rolls, diced

2 eggs, lightly beaten

1 ¼ cups milk

1/2 cup half-and-half

1 tablespoon brandy

1/2 cup sugar

1/4 teaspoon salt

1/2 teaspoon pure almond extract

1/2 teaspoon pure vanilla extract

1/4 teaspoon ground cloves

1/2 teaspoon ground cinnamon

4 tablespoons butter, softened

3/4 cup sugar

1/2 cup almonds, chopped

Directions

Put diced cinnamon rolls into a large-sized bowl.

In a separate bowl or a measuring cup, combine the eggs, milk, half-and-half, brandy, sugar, and salt; now, add almond extract, vanilla extract, cloves, and cinnamon.

Pour the mixture over cinnamon rolls. Let the mixture sit for 10 minutes.

In the third bowl, combine the softened butter, sugar, and almonds using a fork. Divide the bread mixture among 2 mini loaf pans. Top with the almond mixture.

Bake in the air fryer at 310 degrees F for approximately 30 minutes. It will set when it is cooled. Bon appétit!

317. Old-Fashioned Banana Cake

(Ready in about 30 minutes | Servings 4)

Ingredients

Cooking spray

1/4 cup butter

1/3 cup brown sugar

1 banana, mashed

1 egg

2 tablespoons agave nectar

1 cup self-rising flour

1/2 teaspoon cinnamon

A pinch of grated nutmeg

A pinch of kosher salt

Directions

Brush the cake pan with a nonstick cooking spray. In a mixing bowl, beat together the butter and sugar until uniform and creamy.

Then, combine mashed banana, egg, and agave nectar. Now, whisk in the butter mixture; mix until smooth.

Add sifted flour, cinnamon, nutmeg, and salt. Transfer the batter to the cake pan; evenly distribute the batter.

Set the timer for 30 minutes. Now, bake the cake at 320 degrees F until a wooden stick inserted in the center of the cake comes out dry and clean. Enjoy!

318. Coconut Fried Bananas

(Ready in about 10 minutes | Servings 8)

Ingredients

1/2 cup wheat flour	1/2 teaspoon salt
1/2 cup rice flour	3 tablespoons sesame seeds
1 teaspoon baking soda	3 tablespoons sugar
1/2 teaspoon baking powder	4 tablespoons coconut flakes
1/2 cup coconut milk	8 bananas, slice into halves
1 cup water	Icing sugar

Directions

Mix all ingredients, except banana and icing sugar, in a large-sized mixing bowl; stir until well mixed. Dip the banana slices in the batter.

Fry for 6 minutes at 390 degrees F. Dust with icing sugar and serve.

319. Vanilla Cherry Clafoutis

(Ready in about 20 minutes | Servings 6)

Ingredients

2 cups dark red cherries, pitted	A pinch of salt
1/4 cup heavy cream	1 teaspoon pure vanilla extract
1 cup whole milk	1/2 teaspoon pure almond extract
1/2 cup white flour	1/4 teaspoon grated nutmeg
4 eggs	Powdered sugar, for dusting
1/2 cup sugar	

Directions

Lightly grease 2 mini pie pans. Lay the cherries in the pans.

In a saucepan, heat the cream and milk; cook until small bubbles appear around the edges. Now, whisk in the flour.

In a mixing bowl, whisk the eggs, sugar, and salt until the mixture is uniform. Whisk in the cream/milk mixture; add the vanilla extract, almond extract, and nutmeg. Pour this batter over the cherries.

Bake at 330 degrees F for about 20 minutes, or until the top is lightly browned. Dust with powdered sugar and serve warm.

320. Chocolate Mini Cheesecakes

(Ready in about 20 minutes | Servings 8)

Ingredients

For the Crust:

1 cup graham cracker crumbs

2 tablespoons sugar

A pinch of salt

2 ½ tablespoons butter, melted

For the Cheesecake:

2 tablespoons sour cream

1 (8-ounce) package cream cheese, softened

1/3 cup sugar

1 egg

1 teaspoon vanilla extract

1/2 teaspoon ground cinnamon

1 cup chocolate chips

Directions

Line a mini muffin pan with paper liners.

For the Crust: In a medium bowl, mix together all crust ingredients. Divide the crust mixture among prepared muffin cups.

For the Cheesecake: In a mixing bowl, beat together the sour cream, cream cheese, and sugar until uniform and creamy.

Fold in the egg, vanilla extract, and cinnamon. Add 1 tablespoon of chocolate chips to each of the muffin cups.

Now, divide cheesecake batter among eight muffin cups. Lastly, top with the chocolate chips. Bake for 20 minutes at 330 degrees F; bake with batches. Carefully transfer the cheesecakes to a cooling rack.

321. Mini Apple Pies

(Ready in about 25 minutes | Servings 6)

Ingredients

12 wonton wrappers

1/2 cup water

1 tablespoon brown sugar

1/2 teaspoon ground cinnamon

1/4 teaspoon ground cloves

1 teaspoon pure vanilla extract

1 tablespoon flour

4 cooking apples, cored, peeled and sliced

Directions

Prepare a muffin pan by spraying each muffin cup with a nonstick cooking spray; place a wonton wrapper in each muffin cup and press gently.

Next, add other ingredients, except for apples, to a sauce pan; now, cook about 10 minutes. Then, throw in the apples and continue cooking for another 10 minutes or till the apples are soft.

Next, evenly divide the apple mixture among muffin cups. Bake at 350 degrees F for 5 minutes or until the pies are lightly browned. Transfer to a wire rack to cool completely.

322. Strawberry and White Chocolate Muffins

(Ready in about 15 minutes | Servings 8)

Ingredients

1 ½ cups flour

1 teaspoon baking powder

1 teaspoon baking soda

1/2 cup sugar

A pinch of kosher salt

1/3 cup coconut oil, melted

3/4 cup yogurt

1 egg, lightly whisked

1/4 teaspoon ground cloves

1/2 teaspoon ground anise star

1 cup strawberries, quartered

1/2 cup white chocolate bites

Directions

Combine flour, baking powder, baking soda, sugar, and salt in a large-sized mixing bowl. Whisk until you ensure even consistency.

In a separate bowl, mix coconut oil, yogurt, and egg until pale and creamy. Now, add wet to dry mixture; add the cloves and anise star.

Then, gently fold in the strawberries and white chocolate; gently stir to combine. Scrape the batter mixture into muffin cups. Air-fry for 12 minutes at 350 degrees F.

Use a tester to check if they are done. Transfer your muffins to a wire rack to cool completely before serving.

323. Decadent Raisin Bread Pudding

(Ready in about 45 minutes | Servings 6)

Ingredients

6 slices French bread, toasted and diced

1/2 cup half-and-half

1 ¼ cups milk

2 eggs, lightly beaten

1/2 cup brown sugar

1 tablespoon honey

2 tablespoons rum

1/2 teaspoon pure vanilla extract

1/2 teaspoon ground cloves

1/4 teaspoon grated nutmeg

4 tablespoons butter, softened

3/4 cup sugar

1/2 cup raisins, chopped

Directions

Take three mixing bowls. Place diced French bread in a large-sized mixing bowl.

In a separate bowl, combine half-and-half, milk, eggs, brown sugar, honey, rum, and vanilla extract; add the cloves and nutmeg and mix to combine well.

Pour the mixture over the bread. Let it soak for 10 to 15 minutes.

In the third bowl, combine the softened butter with the sugar and raisins. Evenly divide the bread mixture between 2 mini loaf pans. Top with the raisin mixture.

Bake in the air fryer at 310 degrees F for approximately 30 minutes. Bon appétit!

324. Blood Orange and Raspberry Cake

(Ready in about 20 minutes | Servings 6)

Ingredients

For the Cake:

1 cup flour

1/2 cup old-fashioned rolled oats, ground

1/4 cup sugar

1 ½ teaspoons baking powder

1/4 teaspoon grated nutmeg

1/4 teaspoon ground anise star

2 tablespoons unsalted butter

1/2 cup buttermilk

2 large egg whites, lightly beaten

1/2 cup raspberries

For the Glaze:

1/4 cup powdered sugar

1 teaspoon blood orange juice

1 teaspoon vanilla paste

1 teaspoon blood orange peel, finely grated

Directions

Lightly butter 2 mini loaf pans.

Throw the flour, oats, sugar, baking powder, nutmeg, and anise star into a large-sized mixing bowl. Add the butter and mix until mixture resembles coarse crumbs.

Add the buttermilk and egg whites; fold in raspberries. Scrape the butter into the prepared baking pans. Bake at 300 degrees F for 15 minutes.

To make the glaze, mix the powdered sugar with blood orange juice and vanilla paste. Spread the glaze over your cake. To serve: sprinkle with blood orange peel.

325. Country Butter Cake

(Ready in about 30 minutes | Servings 8)

Ingredients

Nonstick cooking spray	1 cup flour
1/2 cup butter	1/2 cup milk
1/2 cup sugar	A pinch of salt
1 egg	1 tablespoon confectioners' sugar

Directions

Treat the cake pan with a nonstick cooking spray. In a mixing dish, beat the butter with the sugar until pale and creamy.

Whisk in the egg; whisk until fluffy. Add the flour, milk, and salt. Transfer the batter to the cake pan; level the surface with a spoon.

Transfer the cake pan to the air fryer. Set the timer to 15 minutes at 350 degrees F. Bake the cake until a tester inserted in the center of the cake comes out dry and clean.

Invert the cake onto a plate and let it stand about 15 minutes. Dust with confectioners' sugar and cut into slices. Serve and enjoy!

326. Hazelnut Tea Cookies

(Ready in about 45 minutes | Servings 6)

Ingredients

5 ounces butter, room temperature

2 ounces powdered sugar

1/3 cup self-rising flour

1/2 cup corn flour

1/2 teaspoon pure almond extract

1/2 teaspoon pure vanilla extract

1/4 cup hazelnuts, finely chopped

Directions

In a mixing dish, beat the butter with powdered sugar until the mixture is fluffy

Add the self-rising flour and corn flour. Now, stir in the almond extract, vanilla and hazelnuts. Mix until you have a soft dough; refrigerate for about 30 minutes.

After that, shape the chilled dough into small balls; transfer them to a baking dish and flatten them with a spoon.

Bake the cookies for 13 minutes at 320 degrees F. Enjoy!

327. Brownies with Hazelnuts and Sultanas

(Ready in about 20 minutes | Servings 4)

Ingredients

3/4 cup chocolate spread

1/4 cup hazelnuts, finely chopped

1/4 cup Sultanas

1 egg

1 tablespoon agave nectar

1/4 cup all-purpose flour

1 teaspoon baking powder

Directions

Begin by mixing all of the above ingredients together. Then, butter a baking pan that will fit in your air fryer.

Scrape mixture into the baking pan. Bake your brownie at 330 degrees F for about 10 minutes. Taste for doneness – it should look set and dry on top. Let it cool for 10 minutes before slicing. Enjoy!

328. Mini Chocolate Strawberry Tartlets

(Ready in about 10 minutes | Servings 10)

Ingredients

20 wonton wrappers

2 eggs, lightly whisked

1 ½ cups chocolate-hazelnut spread

1 cup strawberries, thinly sliced

1 tablespoon melted unsalted butter

1/3 cup granulated sugar

Directions

Brush the edges of each wrapper with the whisked eggs. Divide the chocolate-hazelnut spread among wonton wrapper; divide the strawberries between wrappers.

Next, fold the wrappers diagonally in half over the filling; press and seal the edges.

Add the sugar to a shallow bowl. Grease the wontons with a melted butter; dip each side in the sugar.

Working with batches, place a single layer of your wontons in the air fryer basket. Then, bake at 370 degrees F for 8 minutes, turning over halfway through. Enjoy!

329. Plum and Walnut Rolls

(Ready in about 10 minutes | Servings 8)

Ingredients

2 tablespoons sour cream

8 ounces cream cheese, softened

1/2 cup powdered sugar

1/2 teaspoon pure almond extract

1 teaspoon pure vanilla extract

16 egg roll wrappers

2 cups plums, pitted and chopped

For the Icing:

1/2 cup confectioners' sugar

1/2 walnut, chopped and toasted

2 teaspoons orange juice

2 teaspoons grated orange peel

Directions

Grease a baking pan with a nonstick cooking spray; reserve.

Whip the sour cream, cream cheese, sugar, almond extract, and vanilla extract. Divide the mixture among egg roll wrappers; now, add a small scoop of chopped plums.

Roll the wrappers; press and seal the edges. Transfer the rolls to the prepared baking pan. Bake for about 10 minutes at 375 degrees F, working with batches; turn over halfway through.

In the meantime, combine the ingredients for the icing until blended. Spoon over warm rolls. Bon appétit!

330. Banana Pecan Cobbler

(Ready in about 20 minutes | Servings 4)

Ingredients

4 bananas, sliced

1/2 cup self-rising flour

1/2 cup sugar

1 teaspoon vanilla paste

1/4 teaspoon grated ginger

1 tablespoon cold butter

1/2 cup pecans, chopped

Directions

Arrange the banana slices on the bottom of a baking dish.

In a mixing dish, combine the other items; sprinkle this topping over the banana slices.

Bake at 330 degrees F for about 20 minutes or until golden and bubbly. Serve and enjoy!

331. Fried Banana with Honey-Walnut Sauce

(Ready in about 10 minutes | Servings 4)

Ingredients

1/2 cup flour

2 eggs

3/4 cup breadcrumbs

2 medium-sized bananas, quartered

1 tablespoon powdered sugar

Nonstick cooking spray

1/4 cup honey

1/4 cup walnuts, finely chopped

1/4 teaspoon ground cinnamon

Directions

Prepare three bowls. Place the flour in one of the bowls. In the second bowl, whisk the eggs until foamy; throw the breadcrumbs into the third bowl.

Dust the banana pieces with the powdered sugar. Dip the banana pieces in the flour, then in the egg; lastly, dredge them in the breadcrumbs. Brush them with a cooking spray.

Fry at 350 degrees F for 8 minutes, turning once during the cooking time. Meanwhile, vigorously stir the honey, walnuts, and ground cinnamon. Coat fried banana pieces with the sauce and serve warm.

332. Baked Apples with Chocolate Filling

(Ready in about 30 minutes | Servings 4)

Ingredients

4 cooking apples, cut into halves and cored

1 tablespoon fresh orange juice

1/4 teaspoon grated nutmeg

1/4 teaspoon ground cloves

1/2 teaspoon ground cinnamon

2 tablespoons butter, melted

3 tablespoons granulated sugar

1 (11-ounce) jar chocolate sauce

Directions

Scoop the inside of each apple to make the cavity. Drizzle the apples with the orange juice. Dust each apple with the spices; drizzle with butter and sprinkle with sugar.

Transfer the apples to a baking dish. Bake the apples at 330 degrees F about 30 minutes or until they are tender.

Fill each cavity with the chocolate sauce and serve at room temperature.

333. Cinnamon Almond Cookies

(Ready in about 45 minutes | Servings 10)

Ingredients

4 eggs

1/2 teaspoon pure almond extract

1 teaspoon vanilla paste

1 cup sugar

1 cup canola oil

4 cups flour

1 teaspoon baking powder

1 cup almonds, chopped

A pinch of salt

Cinnamon sugar, for sprinkling

Directions

In a mixing dish, whip together the eggs, pure almond extract, vanilla, sugar, and canola oil.

Next, in a separate dish, sift the flour and baking powder. Add the flour mixture to the egg mixture and mix well to combine.

Stir in the almonds and salt, mixing continuously to combine. Refrigerate for at least 3 hours. Shape the dough into rolls.

Bake at 375 degrees F for about 35 minutes. Cut warm rolls into 1/2-inch thick slices. Sprinkle each slice with cinnamon sugar. Return to your air fryer; bake for an additional 10 minutes.

334. Macadamia and Cranberry Chocolate Dream

(Ready in about 15 minutes | Servings 10)

Ingredients

1 cup chocolate spread

1/2 cup dried cranberries

1/4 cup macadamia nuts, chopped

2 eggs

2 tablespoons honey

1/2 cup all-purpose flour

1 teaspoon baking powder

1/2 teaspoon baking soda

Directions

Thoroughly combine all of the above ingredients together. Then, butter and flour a baking pan.

Spoon the batter into the baking pan. Bake your cake for about 10 minutes at 330 degrees F. Bon appétit!

335. Old-Fashioned Raspberry Muffins

(Ready in about 15 minutes | Servings 8)

Ingredients

1 ½ cups flour

1 teaspoon baking powder

1 teaspoon baking soda

1/2 cup sugar

A pinch of kosher salt

1/3 cup margarine, melted

3/4 cup yogurt

1 egg, lightly whisked

1 teaspoon pure vanilla essence

1/4 teaspoon ground cinnamon

Zest of 1/2 lemon

1 cup fresh raspberries

Coarse sugar for sprinkling

Directions

Take two mixing bowls. In a mixing bowl, combine the flour, baking powder, baking soda, sugar, and salt. Whisk to combine well.

In the second mixing bowl, add the melted margarine, followed by yogurt, egg, vanilla, cinnamon, and lemon zest. Beat until everything is well incorporated.

Now, add wet margarine mixture to dry flour mixture. Then, carefully fold in the fresh raspberries; gently stir to combine.

Scrape the batter mixture into muffin cups. Bake muffins at 350 degrees F for 12 minutes or until the tops are slightly golden brown.

Transfer your muffins to a wire rack to cool completely before serving. Sprinkle some extra coarse sugar over the top of each muffin.

336. Baked Banana with Almonds

(Ready in about 40 minutes | Servings 4)

Ingredients

4 bananas, sliced lengthwise

1/2 teaspoon ground cinnamon

1/4 teaspoon grated nutmeg

1 cup granulated sugar

1/2 teaspoon pure vanilla extract

2 tablespoons cold butter

1/2 cup slivered almonds

Directions

Lightly butter a baking dish; place the banana slices on the bottom of the baking dish.

In a mixing dish, combine the cinnamon, nutmeg, sugar, and vanilla extract. Next, sprinkle the cinnamon mixture over the banana layer.

Cut cold butter into crumbs and scatter them over the layers. Scatter slivered almonds over the top.

Bake for 40 minutes at 375 degrees F. Serve immediately or at room temperature.

337. Butter Coffee Cake with Raspberry Sauce

(Ready in about 25 minutes | Servings 6)

Ingredients

Nonstick cooking spray

1/2 cup butter

1/2 cup sugar

1 egg

1 cup flour

1/2 cup milk

A pinch of salt

1 teaspoon grated orange zest

1 cup frozen raspberries

1/2 cup water

1/2 cup granulated sugar

1 ½ teaspoons cornstarch

Vanilla ice cream, to serve

Directions

Lightly oil the cake pan with a nonstick cooking spray. In a mixing bowl, cream the butter and the sugar until pale and uniform.

Throw in the egg and whip until it is fluffy. Throw in the flour, milk, salt, and orange zest. Scrape the batter into the greased cake pan.

Transfer the cake pan to the air fryer. Bake for 15 minutes at 350 degrees F; use a wooden stick or toothpick to check if the cake is done. Transfer to a wire rack to cool slightly.

In the meantime, make the raspberry sauce by mixing the raspberries, water, and granulated sugar in a sauce pan over medium heat.

When the mixture starts to boil, turn the heat to medium-low; simmer an additional 5 minutes. Strain in order to discard the seeds; pour the strained sauce back into the pan.

Now, whisk in the cornstarch and stir until it's completely dissolved; bring the sauce to a boil. Reduce the heat and simmer another 8 minutes, or until the sauce is syrupy. Drizzle raspberry sauce over the top of your cake. Serve with a dollop of vanilla ice cream.

338. Pecan Chocolate Brownies

(Ready in about 30 minutes | Servings 8)

Ingredients

1 stick butter

8 ounces dark chocolate

4 eggs, lightly whisked

1/2 cup white sugar

1/2 cup brown sugar

1/2 teaspoon pure almond extract

1 teaspoon pure vanilla extract

1/2 cup flour

6 ounces pecan nuts, chopped

Directions

Microwave the butter with the dark chocolate until melted; let it cool.

Beat the eggs with the sugar, almond and vanilla extract.

Next, add the egg mixture to the chocolate mixture. Stir in the flour and pecans. Scrape the batter into the cake pan.

Then, bake the brownies for 30 minutes at 350 degrees F. Taste for doneness and let it cool slightly before slicing and serving.

339. Baked Coconut Peaches

(Ready in about 40 minutes | Servings 4)

Ingredients

Nonstick cooking spray

4 peaches, pitted and quartered

1 cup sugar

1/2 teaspoon ground cloves

1/4 teaspoon ground anise star

1/2 teaspoon pure vanilla extract

1/2 teaspoon pure orange extract

2 tablespoons coconut butter

Coconut flakes, for serving

Directions

Grease the baking dish with a nonstick cooking spray; place the peaches on the bottom of the baking dish.

In a mixing dish, combine the sugar, cloves, anise star, vanilla, and orange extract. Then, sprinkle the sugar/spice mixture over the peach layer.

Cut coconut butter into crumbs and scatter them over the layers. Air-fryer at 375 degrees F for 40 minutes. Serve warm or cold, sprinkled with some extra coconut flakes.

340. Sage and Turmeric Pineapple Fritters

(Ready in about 10 minutes | Servings 6)

Ingredients

2 cups pineapple, cut into chunks

A pinch of salt

1/2 teaspoon turmeric

4 sage leaves, finely minced

1/4 teaspoon ground nutmeg

1 cup flour

1/2 cup milk

2 eggs

Directions

Pulse all ingredients, except the pineapple, in a blender or food processor until smooth and uniform.

Transfer the blended mixture to a mixing bowl; add the pineapple chunks.

Air-fry the battered pineapple chunks for 2 to 3 minutes at 350 degrees F. Work with batches. Dust with icing sugar and serve. Bon appétit!

341. Cherry Cheesecake Wontons

(Ready in about 10 minutes | Servings 8)

Ingredients

2 eggs, lightly whisked

1 cup cream cheese

1/4 cup cherry pie filling

16 wonton wrappers

1/2 cup powdered sugar

1 teaspoon vanilla essence

Melted butter, for brushing

Directions

Brush the edges of each wrapper with the whisked egg. In a mixing dish, combine the cheese with cherry pie filling.

Divide the cream cheese spread among the wrappers. Now, fold the wrappers diagonally in half over the filling; seal the edges with fingertips and fork.

Throw the powdered sugar into a shallow plate; add pure vanilla essence and stir to combine. Brush the wrappers with melted butter; dip the wontons in the vanilla sugar.

Bake at 370 degrees F for 8 minutes, turning over halfway through; work with batches. Bon appétit!

342. Blackberry and Honey Pancakes

(Ready in about 15 minutes | Servings 8)

Ingredients

1 cup blackberries, washed and rinsed

2 tablespoons honey

1 tablespoon orange juice

Pancakes, to serve

Ice cream, to serve

Directions

Add the blackberries to the air fryer pan.

In a mixing dish, combine the honey and the orange juice. Now, drizzle the honey mixture over the top of your blackberries. Cook the berry mixture for 8 minutes at 350 degrees F.

In the meantime, prepare the pancakes according to your favorite recipe or package instructions.

Serve the topping over warm pancakes, garnished with ice cream. Enjoy!

343. Winter Plum and Raisin Dumplings

(Ready in about 25 minutes | Servings 4)

Ingredients

1/4 teaspoon ground cinnamon

1/2 teaspoon nutmeg, preferably freshly grated

1 tablespoon brown sugar

4 tablespoons raisin

4 large-sized plums

4 sheets puff pastry

2 tablespoons butter, melted

Directions

In a mixing dish, thoroughly combine the cinnamon, nutmeg, brown sugar, and raisin.

Place a plum on one puff pastry sheet. Now, add the raisin mixture. Fold the pastry over the filling and seal the edges.

Brush each dumpling with the melted butter. Then, cook your dumplings at 350 degrees F approximately 25 minutes. Bon appétit!

344. Old-Fashioned Dessert Fritters (Beignets)

(Ready in about 1 hour 35 minutes | Servings 12)

Ingredients

1/4 cup sugar

1 ¼ ounces dry yeast

1 egg

1/4 cup buttermilk, warmed

1/4 cup evaporated milk, warmed

A pinch of kosher salt

4 cups flour

1/2 teaspoon baking powder

1/2 teaspoon baking soda

1/4 cup shortening

Confectioners' sugar, for serving

Directions

In a bowl, combine the sugar and yeast; add 3/4 cup of warm water and mix to combine. Let it stand until the mixture becomes foamy.

Add the egg, buttermilk, milk, salt, flour, baking powder, and baking soda; mix to create a dough.

Slowly add the shortening; knead the dough until there are no lumps. Allow the dough to rest, covered, for about 1 hour.

After that, roll the dough until it is 1/2-inch thick. Cut it into squares; transfer the squares to a baking sheet. Let it stand an additional 30 minutes.

Bake at 390 degrees F for 3 to 4 minutes or until done and crispy. Sprinkle with confectioners' sugar and serve.

345. Apple Mint Blueberry Clafouti

(Ready in about 20 minutes | Servings 8)

Ingredients

2 cups fresh blueberries

1/4 cup heavy cream

1 cup whole milk

1/2 cup all-purpose flour

4 eggs

1/2 cup golden caster sugar

A pinch of salt

1 teaspoon pure vanilla extract

1/4 teaspoon ground cardamom

1 teaspoon fresh apple mint, chopped

Icing sugar, for dusting

Directions

Butter two mini pie pans. Lay the blueberries on the bottom of your pans.

In a saucepan, warm the cream together with milk; cook until small bubbles appear around the edges. Now, stir in the flour; continue to cook, stirring with a wire whisk to avoid the lumps.

In a bowl, whisk the eggs, sugar, and salt until the mixture is uniform. Whisk in the cream/milk mixture; add the vanilla extract, cardamom, and apple mint. Pour the batter over the blueberries.

Bake at 330 degrees F for about 20 minutes, or until the top is lightly browned. Garnish with icing sugar and serve warm. Enjoy!

346. Mini Tarts with Caramel Sauce

(Ready in about 30 minutes+ chilling time | Servings 10)

Ingredients

Nonstick cooking spray

20 wonton wrappers

1 cup caster sugar

1 cup thickened cream

1 stick butter, chopped

1 cup pecans

1 ½ tablespoons maple syrup

1/4 teaspoon allspice

Directions

Prepare muffin cups by greasing them with a nonstick cooking spray. Press each wonton wrapper evenly into the center of each cup. Transfer to your air fryer and bake at 350 degrees F for 5 minutes.

Melt the sugar in a saucepan over medium-high flame. Cook for about 5 or until the sugar turns golden. Turn the heat to low.

Next, fold in thickened cream; continue to cook, stirring frequently, approximately 4 minutes or until the cream has thickened. Remove from heat and fold in the butter. Whisk until everything is well incorporated and let the sauce cool slightly.

Meanwhile, preheat your oven to 390 degrees F. Coat a cookie sheet with a baking (parchment) paper.

Mix the pecans, maple syrup and allspice in a bowl. Transfer the pecan mixture to the prepared cookie sheet. Roast them, stirring periodically, for 10 to 12 minutes.

To serve: Pour caramel sauce into the cups. Refrigerate until set; top with maple pecans and serve.

347. Brownies with Cheese and Poppy Seed Swirl

(Ready in about 30 minutes | Servings 10)

Ingredients

8 ounces bittersweet chocolate

8 ounces butter

1 cup caster sugar

4 eggs

1 teaspoon pure hazelnut extract

1 teaspoon pure vanilla extract

1/2 teaspoon ground cinnamon

1/2 teaspoon grated ginger

1 tablespoon cocoa powder, unsweetened

1/2 cup flour

6 ounces walnuts, chopped

2/3 cup cream cheese

2 tablespoons powdered sugar

1 teaspoon grated orange peel

1 egg yolk

1 teaspoon poppy seeds

Directions

Microwave the chocolate together with the butter until it is completely melted.

In a mixing bowl, whip the sugar, eggs, hazelnut extract, vanilla, and spices. Now, add the cocoa powder and flour. Stir in the chocolate mixture followed by chopped walnuts.

Spoon the batter into the baking pan, reserving about 1/2 a cup.

To make the swirl, mix the remaining ingredients in a bowl until smooth, creamy, and uniform. Then, drop large spoonfuls of the swirl onto the brownie batter. Now, top with reserved chocolate batter; swirl with a knife.

Bake for 30 minutes at 350 degrees F. Bon appétit!

348. Festive Chocolate Fig Cake

(Ready in about 15 minutes | Servings 6)

Ingredients

Nonstick cooking spray

1/4 cup caster sugar

1/2 stick softened butter

1 egg

1 tablespoon fig jam

1/2 cup almonds, chopped

2 ounces flour

A pinch of kosher salt

1 ½ tablespoons cocoa powder

Icing sugar, for sprinkling

Directions

Lightly oil a round cake pan with a nonstick cooking spray.

In a mixing bowl, whip the sugar with the butter until light, pale, and creamy. Fold in the egg and fig jam and mix again; now, throw in the almonds and mix again.

Throw in the flour, salt, and cocoa powder. Transfer the batter to the cake pan and bake for 15 minutes at 320 degrees F. Taste for doneness using a wooden stick. Dust with icing sugar and serve.

349. Delicious Macadamia and Raisin Cookies

(Ready in about 45 minutes | Servings 10)

Ingredients

2 ounces muscovado sugar

1 ounce caster sugar

5 ounces butter, room temperature

1/2 cup corn flour

1/3 cup self-rising flour

1 teaspoon pure vanilla extract

1/2 teaspoon ground cinnamon

1/4 teaspoon ground cardamom

2 tablespoons raisins

3 tablespoons macadamia nut, chopped

Directions

In a mixing dish, cream the sugar with butter until the mixture is uniform and fluffy. Sift in the flours. Stir in the vanilla, cinnamon, and cardamom.

Then, add the raisins and macadamia nuts; knead to form a dough; refrigerate for about 30 minutes.

After that, shape the dough into bite-sized balls; transfer them to a baking dish and flatten them using the back of a spoon. Bake the cookies for 13 minutes at 320 degrees F. Bon appétit!

350. Anise Star Plantain Fritters

(Ready in about 10 minutes | Servings 8)

Ingredients

2 cups plantain, peeled and chopped into chunks

1 teaspoon ground anise star

1/2 teaspoon ground cinnamon

1/2 teaspoon vanilla paste

1/4 teaspoon ground nutmeg

1 cup flour

1/2 cup milk

2 eggs

Directions

Mix all ingredients, except the plantain, in a dish until smooth. Then, add the plantain chunks.

Fry the battered plantain chunks for 2 to 3 minutes at 350 degrees F. Work with batches. Dust with cinnamon sugar and serve.

351. Mini Pumpkin Tarts

(Ready in about 20 minutes + chilling time | Servings 10)

Ingredients

Nonstick cooking spray

20 wonton wrappers

1 package cream cheese

1 cup whipped topping

1 cup canned pumpkin pie mix

1/4 teaspoon ground cloves

1/4 teaspoon freshly ground nutmeg

1/2 teaspoon ground cinnamon

1/2 teaspoon grated ginger

Directions

Prepare a muffin pan by spraying it with a nonstick cooking spray. Press each wonton wrapper evenly into the center of each cup.

Transfer to your air fryer and bake at 350 degrees F for 5 minutes. When the edges become golden, they are ready.

Meanwhile, blend all remaining ingredients with an electric mixer; place the cream in the refrigerator until ready to serve.

Once your wonton cups have cooled, divide prepared cream among them. Keep the tarts refrigerated. Bon appétit!

352. Double Chocolate Bread Pudding

(Ready in about 45 minutes | Servings 6)

Ingredients

6 slices Italian bread, cubed

1/2 cup half-and-half

1 ¼ cups milk

2 eggs, lightly beaten

1/2 cup brown sugar

4 tablespoons butter, softened

1/2 cup semisweet chocolate pieces

2 tablespoons unsweetened cocoa powder

1 tablespoon coffee flavored liqueur

1/2 teaspoon pure vanilla extract

1/2 teaspoon ground cloves

Whipped cream, to serve

Directions

Take two bowls. Place cubed bread in the first bowl.

In the second bowl, combine the remaining ingredients, except the whipped cream; mix to combine well.

Pour the chocolate mixture over the bread. Let it soak for 10 to 15 minutes. Evenly divide the mixture between two mini loaf pans.

Bake in the air fryer at 310 degrees F for approximately 30 minutes. Serve chilled with whipped cream. Bon appétit!

353. Chocolate Cashew Cake with Plum Jam

(Ready in about 20 minutes | Servings 6)

Ingredients

1 stick softened butter

1/2 cup sugar

2 eggs, lightly beaten

1/2 cup cashews, chopped

2 tablespoons plum jam

4 ounces flour

2 tablespoons cocoa powder

1/2 teaspoon cinnamon

1/2 teaspoon freshly grated nutmeg

Chocolate frosting, for garnish

Directions

Lightly grease a cake pan with some vegetable oil.

In a mixing dish, whip the butter and sugar until pale and creamy. Fold in the eggs, cashews, and jam; mix again.

Throw in the flour, cocoa powder, cinnamon, and grated nutmeg. Transfer the batter to the cake pan and bake for 15 minutes at 320 degrees F. Taste for doneness using a wooden stick.

Transfer the cake to a wire rack to cool completely. Frost the cake and serve.

354. Mini Blueberry Pies

(Ready in about 25 minutes | Servings 16)

Ingredients

16 wonton wrappers

3/4 cup water

1/4 cup sugar

1/2 teaspoon ground cinnamon

1 teaspoon pure vanilla extract

2 tablespoons flour

1 cup blueberries, cored, peeled and sliced

Directions

Prepare the muffin pan by spraying each muffin cup with some vegetable oil; place a wonton wrapper in each muffin cup and press gently.

Next, add other ingredients, except for blueberries, to a saucepan; cook about 10 minutes over medium heat. Then, throw in the blueberries; reduce the heat to medium-low and continue cooking for another 10 minutes.

Next, evenly divide the blueberry mixture among muffin cups. Bake at 350 degrees F for 5 minutes or until the pies are lightly browned.

Transfer to a cooling rack before serving. Enjoy!

355. Chocolate Strawberry Pound Cake

(Ready in about 25 minutes | Servings 8)

Ingredients

2/3 cup unsalted butter, softened

3 ounces powdered sugar

Zest and juice of 1 orange

3 eggs

2/3 cup flour

1/2 teaspoon baking powder

1 cup chocolate chips

1/2 cup cocoa powder, melted

A pinch of salt

10 strawberries, hulled and sliced

Directions

In a mixing dish, cream the butter, powdered sugar and orange zest using an electric mixer. Fold in the eggs, one at a time; mix until well incorporated.

Next, stir in sieved flour, baking powder, chocolate chips, cocoa powder, orange juice, and a pinch of salt.

Pour batter into the loaf pan. Arrange the strawberries on top of the batter. Bake for 25 minutes at 320 degrees F. Check the cake for doneness and transfer to a wire rack to cool. Enjoy!

356. Chocolate Cherry Tartlets

(Ready in about 10 minutes | Servings 10)

Ingredients

20 wonton wrappers

2 eggs, lightly beaten

1 ½ cups chocolate spread

1 cup cherries, pitted and halved

1 tablespoon unsalted butter, melted

1/3 cup caster sugar

Directions

Brush the edges of each wrapper with the beaten eggs. Divide the chocolate spread among wonton wrappers; divide the cherries between wrappers.

Next, fold the wrappers diagonally in half over the filling; seal the edges with your fingertips.

Then, grease the wontons with a melted butter; dip each side in the caster sugar.

Working with batches, place a single layer of your wontons in the air fryer basket. Then, bake at 370 degrees F for 8 minutes, turning over halfway through. Bon appétit!

357. The Easiest Cinnamon Crispas Ever

(Ready in about 5 minutes | Servings 4)

Ingredients

4 flour tortillas, cut into quarters

1 teaspoon ground cinnamon

2/3 cup powdered sugar

Maple syrup, to serve

Directions

Bake tortilla pieces in your air fryer for about 3 minutes at 350 degrees F.

Combine the cinnamon and sugar in a bag. Add fried tortillas to the cinnamon/sugar mixture; shake until coated well.

Drizzle with maple syrup and serve.

358. Easy Airy Cupcakes

(Ready in about 15 minutes | Servings 8)

Ingredients

1/2 stick butter

1/4 cup caster sugar

1 egg

1/2 cup flour

1 teaspoon pure vanilla extract

3 egg whites

1/2 teaspoon cream of tartar

1 pound confectioners' sugar

Food coloring of choice

Directions

In a mixing bowl, cream the butter with caster sugar until it is fluffy.

Next, fold in the egg and mix to combine; slowly and gradually sift in the flour; add vanilla extract. Divide the batter among the lined muffin cups and bake for 8 minutes at 330 degrees F.

Meanwhile, prepare the topping. Using an electric mixer, beat the egg whites and cream of tartar until foamy.

Next, gradually add the confectioners' sugar, and continue mixing until stiff glossy peaks form. Add the food coloring and stir until color is even. Decorate your cupcakes and serve.

359. Easy Father's Day Flan

(Ready in about 40 minutes | Servings 4)

Ingredients

1 tablespoon melted butter

1/3 cup sugar

2 tablespoons water

1 1/3 cups evaporated milk

1/4 cup sweetened condensed milk

3 eggs

1 egg yolk

1 teaspoon vanilla extract

Directions

Lightly coat four ramekins with melted butter.

In a saucepan, cook the sugar and water for 10 minutes over medium-high heat, swirling the saucepan constantly.

Now, pour 1 tablespoon of the warm caramel into the bottom of each ramekin.

In a bowl, make the custard by whisking the milk with the eggs and egg yolk; add vanilla extract and stir again. Scrape the custard into the ramekins.

Bake, covered, for 30 minutes at 320 degrees F. Serve well chilled.

360. White Chocolate Croissant Bread Pudding

(Ready in about 45 minutes | Servings 8)

Ingredients

8 croissants, diced

2 eggs, lightly beaten

1 ¼ cups milk

1 cup half-and-half

1/2 cup sugar

A pinch of salt

1/2 teaspoon pure almond extract

1/2 teaspoon ground cinnamon

4 tablespoons butter, softened

3/4 cup powdered sugar

10 ounces good-quality white chocolate, coarsely chopped

Directions

Put diced croissants into a large-sized bowl.

In a separate bowl, whisk the eggs, along with the milk, half-and-half, sugar, and salt; now, add almond extract and cinnamon.

Pour the mixture over the croissants. Let it soak for 10 to 15 minutes.

In the third bowl, combine the butter, powdered sugar, and white chocolate. Divide the bread mixture among 2 mini loaf pans. Top with the chocolate mixture.

Bake in the air fryer at 310 degrees F for approximately 30 minutes. It will set when it is cooled. Enjoy!

361. Country-Style Peach Dessert

(Ready in about 30 minutes | Servings 8)

Ingredients

1/4 cup butter

1/3 cup sugar

2 peaches, pitted and mashed with a fork

1 egg

2 tablespoons honey

1 cup flour

1 teaspoon baking powder

A pinch of kosher salt

1/2 teaspoon ground anise star

1/2 teaspoon apple pie spice

Directions

Firstly, coat the cake pan with a thin layer of vegetable oil. In a mixing bowl, beat together the butter and sugar until fluffy and creamy.

Now, add mashed peaches, egg, and honey. Now, whisk in the butter mixture; mix again.

Sift in the flour, baking powder, kosher salt, anise star, and apple pie spice. Ladle the batter into the cake pan; evenly distribute the batter using the back of a spoon.

Bake for about 30 minutes at 320 degrees F. Taste for doneness and transfer to a cooling rack before serving.

362. Honey-Baked Tangy Apricots

(Ready in about 40 minutes | Servings 4)

Ingredients

8 apricots, pitted and halved

1/2 cup honey

1/4 teaspoon ground anise star

1/2 teaspoon pure vanilla extract

1/2 teaspoon key lime extract

1 teaspoon crystallized ginger

Chilled heavy cream, to serve

Directions

Coat a baking dish with a thin layer of vegetable oil or coconut butter; place the apricots on the bottom of the baking dish.

In a mixing dish, combine all ingredients, except heavy cream. Top apricot layer.

Bake at 375 degrees F for 40 minutes. Serve cold garnished with chilled heavy cream.

363. Winter Plum and Walnut Dessert

(Ready in about 40 minutes | Servings 4)

Ingredients

Nonstick cooking spray

8 plums, pitted and halved

1 cup caster sugar

1/2 cup ground walnuts

1/4 teaspoon ground anise star

1/2 teaspoon pure vanilla extract

2 tablespoons coconut butter

Raisins, to serve

Directions

Lightly grease a baking dish with a cooking spray; arrange the plums on the bottom of the baking dish.

In a mixing dish, combine the sugar, walnuts, anise star, and vanilla extract. Then, sprinkle the walnut mixture over the plum layer.

Cut coconut butter into crumbs and scatter them over the layers. Bake at 375 degrees F for 40 minutes. Serve warm or cold sprinkled with raisin.

364. Coconut and Plum Pound Cake

(Ready in about 35 minutes | Servings 10)

Ingredients

1/2 cup coconut butter

1/2 cup sugar

1 cup all-purpose flour

1 egg

1/2 cup milk

1 teaspoon grated orange zest

1/4 cup coconut flakes

1 cup frozen plums, pitted and chopped

1/2 cup water

1/2 cup caster sugar

1/2 teaspoon ground cinnamon

2 tablespoons cornstarch

Directions

Grease a cake pan with some vegetable oil. In a mixing bowl, beat the butter and the sugar until pale and uniform.

Fold in the egg and whip until it is fluffy. Now, add the milk, orange zest, and coconut flakes. Spoon this batter into the cake pan.

Transfer the cake pan to the air fryer. Bake for 15 minutes at 350 degrees F; use a tester to check if the cake is done. Transfer to a wire rack to cool slightly.

In the meantime, make the sauce by mixing the plums, water, caster sugar and cinnamon in a saucepan over medium heat.

When the mixture starts to boil, turn the heat to medium-low; simmer an additional 5 minutes.

Whisk in the cornstarch and stir until it's completely dissolved; bring the sauce to a boil. Reduce the heat and simmer another 8 minutes, or until the sauce is syrupy. Drizzle the plum sauce over your cake. Serve sprinkled with some extra coconut flakes. Enjoy!

365. One-More-Bite Flan

(Ready in about 55 minutes + chilling time | Servings 6)

Ingredients

3/4 cup caster sugar

8 ounces cream cheese, softened

5 eggs

1 (14-ounce) can sweetened condensed milk

1 (12-ounce) can evaporated milk

Directions

In a heavy saucepan, stir caster sugar over medium-low heat until melted, or about 15 minutes. Quickly pour the melted sugar into prepared ramekins, tilting to coat the bottom; allow them to stand for about 10 minutes.

In a mixing bowl, beat the cream cheese until smooth; then, fold in the eggs, one at a time, and beat to combine well.

Pour in the milk and mix again. Pour the mixture over caramelized sugar. Bake, covered, for 30 minutes at 320 degrees F. Refrigerate overnight; invert the custards onto platters; garnish with berries and serve.

Download a PDF file with photos of all the recipes from the link below

75189369R00110

Made in the USA
Columbia, SC
12 August 2017